The Turning Points

1965 WAR

TO FIND US YOU MUST BE GOOD

TO CATCH US YOU MUST BE FAST

TO BEAT US

YOU MUST BE KIDDING

The Turning Points
1965 WAR

Sonnia Singh

KW Publishers Pvt Ltd
New Delhi

ISBN 978-93-89137-69-9 Paperback

Published in India by Kalpana Shukla

KW Publishers Pvt Ltd
4676/21, First Floor, Ansari Road
Daryaganj, New Delhi 110002
Phone: +91 11 23263498/43528107
Marketing: kw@kwpub.com
Editorial: production@kwpub.com
Website: www.kwpub.com

I would like to dedicate this book to:

My Parents—My lifeline—Brigadier Surinder and Neena—You always encouraged me to do my best and introduced me to the lovely world of books.

Thank you for the numerous sacrifices you have made for all your children with so much love.

The stories in the *Turning Points* are a tribute and homage to the soldiers and officers of the Indian Armed Forces who fought valiantly in the line of duty despite all odds and kept the tricolor flying high. These noble acts are what ensure our freedom today for had the agenda set by the enemy been achieved the consequences are unthinkable. We salute the sacrifices, the invincible grit and indomitable spirit of these heroes—Yes, Heroes live amongst us.

Contents

... AND TO THE PLAINS OF PUNJAB

Foreword

India-Pakistan War of 1965 had many surprises for both sides. From Rann of Kutch, to large-scale infiltration into Jammu and Kashmir and finally an offensive in the Chhamb-Jourian sector, all caught India by surprise. While India, in each case, quickly overcame the shocks from these surprise actions by Pakistan, Her own offensives both in the Punjab and Jammu sectors took Pakistan completely by surprise and the latter could not fully recover from these setbacks.

Pakistan was under the impression that the Indian Army, consequent to the drubbing it received at the hands of Chinese Army, was in poor shape and would refrain from reacting to Pakistan's moves. This assessment by Pakistan led to many missteps by it. Pakistan first made attempts at some ingress into Indian territory in the Rann of Kutch area, in the hope that India as a reaction to this would shift more of its military to that sector of its Country. India did not react to this move by Pakistan in the way they expected. This came to be Pakistan's first miscalculation.

Next Pakistan sent a large body of infiltrators into J&K in the hope that their arrival in the valley will lead to a large-scale revolt by the local population. Once that happened, Pakistan Army could move in and take control of the better part of J&K and eventually the whole of the state. "Bakarwalas" passed the information of this infiltration and the Indian Army reacted with alacrity and dispatch. Not only did India successfully evict these infiltrators, but She even captured the strategically important Haji Pir Pass. Thus, Pakistan's second mischief too came to be effectively negated by the Indian Army.

Having failed in these two attempts, Pakistan went in for the third, in which it mounted a full-scale offensive in the Chhamb–Jourian sector, where it had distinct advantage, under the impression that since it is across the Line of Control (LoC) in Jammu and Kashmir territory, India too will react across the LoC only. Pakistan did make some progress in this offensive in the Chhamb sector, but was soon checkmated by the Indian troops. This turned out to be the third miscalculation on the part of Pakistan because India, instead of reacting on her side of the LoC, decided to mount an offensive across the international border. Thus started the 1965 India-Pakistan War.

Consequent to the 1962 War with China, the Indian Army's focus had shifted to the Tibet border and consequent reorganisation of its Army so as to be able to fight in high mountains. In addition, the Army's equipment, particularly the armour, was of Second World War vintage. India had only four regiments equipped with Centurion tanks, which alone could stand its ground against Pakistan's Patton tanks.

Since India had no obstacle system of its own to base defences, it decided to make use of Pakistan's obstacles. On the Punjab front the plan was to advance up to the Ichhogil Canal, short of Lahore and base defences on it. On the Jammu front the plan was similar, in that the advance was up to Marala-Ravi link canal, and base own defences on this obstacle. On both fronts, the strategy was to establish a few bridgeheads across these obstacles and let Pakistan expend its offensive potential against these. Since Centurion was the only tank with India which could stand up to Pakistan's Patton tank, one regiment of Centurions was left for the Punjab front, while the rest of the Indian Armoured division (with three Centurion regiments) was deployed on the Jammu front. India had no option except to deploy mountain infantry divisions (neither equipped nor trained for warfare in the plains) in the plains of Punjab and J&K during this War.

The War lasted only a few weeks, and in this short period of time, the Indian Army crippled Pakistan's tank fleet and destroyed its Army's offensive potential. When the War ended the Indian Army was decidedly and decisively on top. This was so notwithstanding Pakistan Army's decided advantage in its tank fleet, better artillery guns, and fighting on interior lines. During this short War, there were innumerable cases of excellent performance by individual units as well as exceptional acts of bravery by both officers and men.

The Indian Army also carried out a few operations in parts of J&K to forestall any mischief by Pakistan. These included ones in the HAJI PIR pass area, POONCH and URI sectors, as well as in KRISHAN GANGA/NEELAM river area.

Every battle and every War has a few turning points, where the scales can tilt on either side. Sonnia, being one with little or no direct interaction with Military has been able to put together with great accuracy, remarkable skill and detail, a series of such turning points during the 1965 War between India and Pakistan. She has brought to light actions of units and individuals in painstaking detail and sensitivity. Not to miss the daredevil actions of the pilots of Indian Air Force and the sterling role they played in this War, she has highlighted their extraordinary performance and individual acts of bravery.

It is indeed a remarkable effort for a young girl to undertake the task of putting together in such detail the stories of an individual's bravery and the sterling performance of the units of the Indian Army: their spirit and determination to surmount impossible odds.

She has been able to piece together these stories for the layperson and to apprise him (and her) of the ups and downs of this War. Let him (and her) know of the men who put their lives on the line, in the line of duty—Duty of which the lord spoke so eloquently to a wavering Arjuna on the battlefield of KURUKSHETRA.

It is a book which every Indian needs to read to know of the men and their leaders who thought nothing of their own lives when the safety of their country was as stake.

Jai Hind!

Lt. Gen Harwant Singh PVSM, AVSM

Prologue

The India-Pakistan War of 1965

The year 1965 saw India and Pakistan engaged in a prolonged War. It was not a continuous War, rather a series of conflicts between India and Pakistan and was the second War fought over Kashmir. A deliberate breach of the borders by Pakistan along the ceasefire line ended up with the city of Lahore almost being captured by a jubilant Indian Army just 13 km away from the city!

It may be noted that Lieutenant General Harbaksh Singh, VRC was the Army Commander of the Western Command, in whose area of responsibility the War was fought. Capt. Amarinder Singh (current CM of Punjab) then a young captain in the Sikh Regiment (2 SIKH) was his aide de camp (ADC).

There was no formal declaration of War—it was initiated by Pakistan Armed Forces inching into India through subterfuge initially in the Rann of Kutch followed by full combat in the Akhnoor area. The largest tenure of the battle was 22 days.

The War commenced on April 8, 1965 and ended by a ceasefire announcement on September 22, 1965. There were three armed incursions by Pakistan Armed Forces into India's territory covertly and boldly with the primary intent of conquering Kashmir and thereafter bringing other terrain spoils into their custody. Pakistan Army was certain of victory as they believed that India would not be able to defend Herself after Her then recent loss to China in 1962 and they assumed it to be an easy conquest. The statement made was "Breakfast in Lahore, Lunch in Amritsar and Dinner at Delhi"—"Chalo Kashmir" was their motto.

In terms of global relations, Iran, Indonesia and China gave ample political support to Pakistan at the time. However, the Pakistan military was in for a rude shock when their sole arms supplier was unwilling to enter this conflict—the United States of America chose to remain neutral. So did the Soviet Union, which was a big blow to India. The *Modus Operandi* deployed by Pakistan under the leadership of PM were as:

Phase One: Operation Dessert Hawk

Field Marshall Ayub Khan wanted the Indian Forces attention diverted away from Kashmir so he deliberately chose the Rann of Kutch as the first encroachment point. India responded with "Operation Kabaddi" in a terrain of Her own choosing. This incursion of Pakistan Forces seemed to have been a testing ground for Pakistan's military to gauge the armour and mettle of India.

The Indian troops had been moved to the Western border (*Operation Ablaze*) and were deployed on the Punjab border—a move that was not anticipated by the other side. Unknown to Pakistan, India made one alteration on her side—due to the foresight of the Army Commander, one Armoured Division of the Army remained stationed around Jullundur-Kapurthala-Kartarpur area.

By June 1965 UK PM Harold Wilson intervened and exerted international pressure and the *Kutch-Sind pact* was signed in July 1965, and status quo maintained as territories were handed back by both sides. PM Shastri and General Ayub were to meet on August 20th for discussions as General Ayub had cited being extremely busy before that—busy planning his next invasion on India, as it came about.

Phase 2: Operation Gibraltar

On August 5, 1965, between 26,000 and 33,000 Pakistani soldiers and trained infiltrators crossed the Line of Control (LOC) dressed as local Kashmiris and blended into various regions of Kashmir—the master plan being that they would merge with the local populace and instigate them against the Indian Government. Pakistan was smart in using infiltrators so that She could proclaim to the world that these were not Her military and had no hand in these insurgent operations. Then, after stirring the natives towards an uprising, it was envisaged that Pakistan Forces would storm in—supposedly to answer the appeal of local citizens to free them from India! The plan of the infiltrators was to have an open revolt by using the celebrations of "Pir Dastagir Sahib" on August 8, 1965 to mingle in and then capture the radio station and airfield. This was the modus operandi of Operation Gibraltar.

The infiltration was preceded by acts of arson and firing along the CFL. Initially, the Indian side did not take these as seriously as they should have. When these got intense and reinforcements were asked for it took a long while to come, by which time War had already erupted. Luckily, and unapparent to Pakistan Army, the locals became wary of these new faces burgeoning by the dozen and tipped the Indian Forces who rallied and prepared for the defence of their territories and then planned to give a resounding answer to the enemy.

Operation Gibraltar was a total failure as the element of surprise that would have rendered the Indian side defenseless and being caught off guard could not be achieved and the Pakistani incendiary cover was blown. The strategy and training of the infiltrator force was apparently done under the command of Maj. Gen. Hussain Malik, 12 INF DIV.

Phase 3: Operation Grand Slam

On September 1, 1965, Pakistan launched a counterattack after India took tactical measures to gain enemy territory. It was called *Operation Grand Slam* to counter the failure of *Operation Gibraltar.* The aim was to capture Akhnoor and subsequently Jammu in the Chhamb sector. It was a bold move as this action would have cut off communications and supplies to Indian Forces. This plan also included camp set-ups in Khem Karan sector by Pakistan Forces with the intent of encircling Amritsar. Maj. Gen. Hussain Malik of 12 INF DIV was overall in-charge. The plan was drawn up as early as May 1965 and focused on the entry to India vide Akhnoor, Jammu and then Kashmir. This too was countered and failed miserably. Thereafter India took the initiative and shifted the battleground to Punjab and Sialkot sectors and thrust into enemy territory despite differing world opinion.

The initial battles were confined to the Infantry Battalions and Armoured Regiments from both sides. The Air Force too got into the thick of it due to the foresight of the then Marshal of the Indian Air Force Arjan Singh. India started with a defensive position and after retaliating went on the offensive. The largest engagement was in Sialkot region. Rapid developments got the Indian Forces within range of Lahore Airport!

Closure

By September 22 both sides had agreed to a UN mandated ceasefire and the War ended in a stalemate. It is believed that had India not succumbed to International pressure for a cease-fire, it would have won the War. Marshal of the Indian Air Force Arjan Singh had advised PM Lal Bahadur Shastri not to agree for ceasefire but it went unheeded. It should be noted that Pakistan Armed Forces had a qualitative edge in air power and armour over India at that time. Their strength too was numerically superior but at the time of ceasefire India held more enemy territory in Her fold.

Note

India's leadership unfortunately did away on the negotiating table what the gallant soldiers had won on the battlefield—all to show a sense of fair play which did not bring any goodwill from the neighbour. India held 1,920 square km of Pakistan territory as against a mere 550 square km of Indian land held by Pakistan. Despite the Haji Pir Pass (had this remained with India, as it rightly should have, then it would have negated Pakistan's dominance in the region and thwarted any future excursions into Indian territory) being captured by the Indian soldiers by sheer grit and huge sacrifices and definitely called for a resounding victory—India surrendered everything at the Tashkent Declaration in January 1966.

Prelude to the War

The Situation & Condition in India in 1965

The Sino-Indian conflict of 1962 had resulted in a devastating defeat for India. This in turn forced the Indian Army to re-evaluate its Armour and Strategy. India found an ally in the Soviet Union when it scouted for military modernisation, and in time to come Russia became the primary arms supplier to India. India till date remains committed to a policy of Peace and the initiative to launch an offensive action remains with the enemy. In mid-1965, the Indian Army was still in the midst of raising a new Corps, and many fresh cadets were still getting trained.

Pakistan, on the other hand, had received a considerable amount of American military aid at this time giving them confidence in their armed potential. Pakistan had also strategically bolstered the Ichhogil canal area—a natural advantage for them as it was situated between River Ravi and River Sutlej—and a huge obstacle for the Indian Forces should they have ever considered an approach from this direction. From an Army man's angle a water canal is a natural defensive structure that offers the dual advantage of not only economising their own forces but it also thwarts the advance of an enemy by limiting manoeuvrability.

Pakistan colluding with China had also soured Indo-Pakistan relations. Pakistan was counting on China to keep India well engaged in the Eastern sector thereby giving them an opportunity to attack in the Western Frontier. This situation coupled with their nascent shopping spree for military equipment was an ideal stage set for their sure-fire victory. Except for two gross miscalculations—the first being Pakistan's presumption of China as an ally alongside which did not happen as China made no contribution to the conflict (at that time

China's leadership was in disarray and the world was unaware of it) and, secondly—the more serious one—that of underestimating the mettle of the Indian Forces.

The Indian Forces were seriously in poor shape. The new raisings had still not been completed, and most of the troops were still undergoing training when they were called in to take action! These new formations were not even provided with the required equipment and the Army units were constantly short of equipment and machinery during the War. The Pakistan Army of 352 Patton tanks (M47s and M48s with a 90 mm gun—the most advanced tanks of that time), 308 Shermans and 96 Chafees pitted against the Indian 186 Centurions, 332 Shermans and 90 AMX-13s were a dismal story to begin with. The Indian tanks and guns should have been phased out a while back and replenished with more sophisticated tanks and machines. Bottom line, Pakistan Army was truly a force to be reckoned with at that time.

On the Airforce front, IAF was equipped with Gnats and Mystères which were no match for the superiority of the Starfighters possessed by the Pakistan Air Force. The Gnats though were better when pitted against the Pakistani Sabres—a fact not considered by the other side. The gist of it is that in calculating a sure win "the Pakistan strategists were mathematically correct" but the "human element" was not factored in the equation.

And lastly, India still needed to guard her frontiers against China. So, India was not in a state to go to War but was compelled to do so. Lt. Gen. Harbaksh Singh, when he took over the Western Command, was a seasoned military warrior and a great military strategist. He had considerable experience in the 1947-48 War and many international missions. His astute assessment of the situation in 1965 and detailed planning were responsible for turning the invasion around in three broad phases, namely, defending the invaded areas, taking measures swiftly to check the infiltrators, and then launching an offensive. A thoroughly planned checkmate.

Modus Operandi of India

Phase 1: Operation Kabbadi (Defensive Strategy)—Ebb the flow of infiltrators and stop all transgressions. Ensure the security of the borders in Punjab and Rajasthan as well.
Phase 2: Operation Ablaze—Stabilise the situation and move reinforcements and resources. To ensure lines of communication remain intact. Continue defending Ladakh in case of Chinese aggression.
Phase 3: Operation Riddle (Offensive Strategy)—Mount combat operations with the aim of securing territory east of River Ravi including capture of Lahore if possible.

Sequence of Events—1965

(Excerpts from The War Despatches written by Lt. Gen. Harbaksh Singh)

April 9, 1965: Crossing of International border by Pakistan Army under Operation Dessert Hawk.
May 1965: Operation Kargil launched by the Indian Army.
June 1965: Ceasefire (pressure tactics by PM Wilson, UK) and withdrawal from occupied territories by both India and Pakistan.
August first week 1965: Infiltrators sneak into Kashmir (unknown to India) through multiple points under Operation Gibraltar.
August 5, 1965: Indian Army informed about presence of infiltrators in separate incidents by locals—the military intelligence had no idea of their presence.
August 8, 1965: On the political front, the Indian Army was asked to take control of J&K but declined. It became an advantageous decision in time to come as else the enemy would have used that situation too to cite dissatisfaction by the people of Kashmir and conveniently march into the region under the pretext of helping the Kashmiris. In Srinagar as many as 2,000 infiltrators had sneaked in and had grand plans to take over the *Srinagar* Airfield. The Army Commander reshuffled positions of units. 63 INF BDE from *Leh* was asked to come down. 4 SIKH LI

was scheduled to fly from *Ambala* as reinforcements but unfortunately could not land due to bad weather and had to deplane at *Pathankot*. 2/9 GORKHA who had reached from *Jammu* that night dived straight into action as the infiltrators started shooting. There was action along CFL the entire night.

August 9, 1965: The infiltrators occupied the track from *Mandi* town leading to *Poonch*. South of *Mandi* town, *Sunderbani* Area was well entrenched with infiltrators who set about destroying bridges which halted the progress of the Indian troops at *Kargil*.

August 10, 1965: 63 INF BDE from *Leh* arrived by road and 4 SIKH LI could land in *Srinagar*. More than a hundred infiltrators in *Chhamb* area engaged the Indian troops in gun fire.

August 11, 1965: An offensive strategy was approved for the Indian Army and the focus of the strategy was to capture the *Haji Pir* and Kishanganga bulges. In *Mandi*, 8 GRENADIERS launched a strong offensive and cleared the heights guarding the town. 191 INF BDE came under heavy enemy shelling at night which was countered successfully.

August 12, 1965: Indian troops moved covertly for *Chor Pinjal* range. 1 MADRAS cleared Point 4007. *Mandi* was captured by 52 MTN BDE. This was the first turn-around. The night saw incessant firing in *Poonch* and *Srinagar* sectors.

August 13, 1965: 8 KUMAON battalion base at *Naugam* was attacked. The Commanding Officer (CO), Lt. Col. Gore, was killed in action. The convoy evacuating the unit was also ambushed. This was a setback for everyone. 4 SIKH LI deployed at *Baramulla*.

August 14, 1965: SRI force came into being and were straightaway put to work to deal with infiltrators. This freed 19 INF DIV to prepare and launch the offensive. India's pleas to UN went unheeded as they refused to intervene because Pakistan had propagated that Kashmiris were waiting to be liberated and they shrewdly denied any involvement with the infiltrators. International media propagation was a tactic deployed effectively by Pakistan Army.

August 15, 1965: Pakistan Army, now no longer in covert operations, shelled the Indian post at *Dewa* and succeeded in blowing up an ammunition dump causing heavy casualties. At this point. Brig. Manmohan Singh who was commanding 162 INF BDE (under 26 INF DIV) was asked to immediately move to *Jourian* to take over 191 INF BDE. Due to this grave situation the *Haji Pir* offensive was postponed. *Gati* Picquet which had been valiantly combating enemy fire for over a week had run out of arms and supplies—they had been cut off for more than 7 days and had to abandon their post. They had fought without food and water since August 10! *Udhampur* area came under heavy enemy attack that night.

August 16, 1965: Pakistan Army openly intruded into Indian territory—in their uniforms this time. Entry through *Pharkian Di Gali.*

August 17, 1965: Infiltrators trespassed into *Miransahib.*

August 18, 1965: Army readied for offensive launch. 68 INF BDE was tasked to advance to *Haji Pir* and link up with reinforcements at *Poonch.* 104 INF BDE was tasked with destroying the Mirpur bridge and clearance of areas. Heavy clashes that night in *Uri* and *Srinagar* areas. 2 SIKH secured a firm base west of *Dewa.*

August 19, 1965: Enemy fire in *Poonch* rendered the airfield unfit for flying. However, the damaged landing ground was repaired the same evening.

August 20, 1965: 2 SIKH achieved their objective and captured the *Green Ridge* and *Red Hill.* 6/5 GORKHAS secured *Point 3779.*

August 21, 1965: *Jammu* was infested with a large number of infiltrators (300-400). *Haji Pir* POA was set for 27th night. Heavy shelling in *Uri* sector continued. An enemy intrusion into *Tithwal* sector was successfully repulsed by the Indian contingent.

August 22, 1965: Air violations by Pakistan Air Force commenced in *Bandipur* and *Sopian.* Air Force base at *Cholibat* was hit.

August 23, 1965: Infiltrators were cleared from areas up till *Kulan.* 2 RAJPUT and 3/8 GORKHA RIFLES secured the "Ring contour" across CFL as per plan.

August 24, 1965: India launched the *Haji Pir* offensive code named "Operation Bakshi" from *Uri* as well as *Poonch* as per plan. But at the last minute had to be deferred to 25th due to the torrential downpour which inhibited progress through the canals. 1 SIKH was tasked with carrying out the offensive in *Tithwal.* 2 RAJPUT and 3/8 GORKHAS attacked enemy post at night led by Maj. Kapur causing the enemy to flee in confusion. By 2250 hrs *Runnar Ridge* was with Indian troops.

August 25, 1965: D-Day for *Haji Pir* offensive. Launched along *Uri-Haji Pir* pass by 19 INF DIV. At night, *Pir Sahiba* feature was attacked by 2 RAJPUT and Nauseri bridge destroyed.

August 26, 1965: 1 PARA commenced attack on *Sank* as part of Operation Bakshi at 2130 hrs. 6 BIHAR captured *Mehendi Gali.*

August 27, 1965: 1 PARA reached the peak at 0415 hrs and caught the enemy by surprise. They added the capture of *Sank* to their victory. Then they carried on without resting to *Sar* and captured it too at 0930 hrs. Two hrs later *Ladi wali Gali* also fell to them. Despite the exhaustion they carried forth to *Haji Pir.*

August 28, 1965: *Haji Pir* was in Indian custody at 1030 hrs. 19 PUNJAB finally achieved success as *Bedori* fell into their hands.

August 30, 1965: Indian troops pressed on into Pakistan territory and captured *Point 8786.*

August 31, 1965: Pakistan Army carried out heavy shelling in desperation from *Red Hill* on the villages of *Mandiala* and *Chhamb.* At 0830 hrs Pakistan Army made a foray with Patton tanks. 20 LANCERS of the Indian Army sent them packing. Another breach by Pakistan Army took place in *Mandiala* with Patton tanks and they were successful in driving a wedge between *Mandiala* and *Chhamb* by nightfall.

September 1, 1965: Enemy running amuck in Indian territory. They had launched "Operation Grand Slam." Good defence put up by Indian Forces. Orders were received by 191 INF BDE to withdraw to *Akhnoor.* 41 Mountain BDE occupied Jourian-Troti sector.

September 3, 1965: At 1915 hrs enemy forces mounted attack on *Jourian.*

September 4, 1965: 161 Field Regiment abandoned their guns and caused a huge setback to the advances made by the Indian Army. Pakistan ignored the UN calls for ceasefire as they were on a high with this victory. The Indian Army decided to mount an offensive in

Sialkot area. Shifting of troops and all forward movements were done by dusk—within 9 hrs.

September 5, 1965: Offence plan for *Khem Karan-Kalra* sector. Shifting of defence lines to *Ichhogi* canal with dual purpose of security of Punjab and capturing enemy territory whilst diverting the enemy from *Akhnoor* area. *Operation Ablaze* was set for September 7. However, troops were aligned west of the river to prepare for attack the next day instead of September 7. Punjab police roped in to broadcast that no one move out of their houses to ensure civilian safety.

September 6, 1965: XI Corps crossed the Radcliffe line into Punjab, causing the enemy to pull out of *Chhamb* sector. *Operation Ablaze* was advanced by a day due to unexpected turn of events in *Chhamb*. H Hour moved to 0400 hrs. GOC 15 INF DIV caused the situation to slip because of a negative mindset and not inspiring his men due to which 38 INF DIV had covered only 2,000 yards and 54 INF BDE was inert. 48 INF BDE commenced advance with 6/8 GORKHA and captured *Nurpur* village but suffered heavy casualties and so handed over to 65 INF BDE. 17 RAJPUT crossed the IB as per plan and prevented further enemy ingress.

September 7, 1965: Enemy attempts at different areas to foray into Indian side were successfully repulsed. 7 GRENADIERS and two Coys of 1/9 GORKHA RIFLES had abandoned their positions—a big hurdle to the other Indian units. At 0930 hrs 9 JAK RIFLES was strafed by enemy fire. The Commanding Officer and Coys withdrew without permission shamefully leaving the rest of the battalion to its fate. The deserting act of 13 DOGRA had an impact on 4 MTN DIV operations which had to be replaced. The GOC of 15 INF DIV was relieved of his command due to deteriorating morale of the men under him. Maj. Gen. Mahinder Singh took over, but this situation had given the enemy the necessary time to react.

September 8, 1965: 13 PUNJAB and 15 DOGRA (of 54 INF BDE) abandoned their defences and caused a huge blow to the men on the front lines. 96 INF DIV was called in to take over. Battle of *Assal Uttar* launched by Pakistan at 1430 hrs and repulsed by 9 HORSE.

September 9, 1965: 17 SIKH arrived from *Ambala* and joined the battle.

September 10, 1965: Battle of *Phillora* commenced. Battle of *Barki.* 16 PUNJAB were pushing east of the Ichhogil canal and at 2340 hrs achieved their objective. 1 JAT and 6 KUMAON in *Ranian* withdrew and it fell to the enemy.

September 11, 1965: India emerged victorious in the Battle of *Asal-Uttar*. Post the capture of *Barki* 4 SIKH were also told to cross the tanks over *Barki* drain. Barki was 14 km from *Lahore*. Instead of enveloping *Lahore* 4 SIKH were sent to *Khem Karan* despite being fatigued and not having slept for two days but had to take this on due to abandonment of the earlier mentioned units. They unfortunately walked into an enemy tank harbour en route and were captured by the enemy.

September 12, 1965: India emerged victorious in the Battle of *Phillora.*

September 17, 1965: 3 KUMAON conducted assault on enemy position at *Gulaba Chhapar* but were unable to hold on.

September 19, 1965: 3 KUMAON attacked *Keri* at 0300 hrs but withdrew to point 2030 due to heavy counter-firing.

September 20, 1965: *MEGHDOOT* force penetrated 4,000 yards into enemy territory at *Thil.* Struck at *Nathal,* 80 miles behind enemy lines.

September 23, 1965: Ceasefire announced.

October 5, 1965: *Point 3776* in *Kalidhar ridge* cleared by 6 SIKH LI.

October 15, 1965: *Jura Bridge* in *Kishanganga, Tithwal area ridge* cleared by 4 KUMAON.

November 3, 1965: *Operation Hill* recaptured by 6 SIKH LI.

Acknowledgements

The Warriors—of the 1965 War—who fought valiantly and patiently recounted the twists and turns of some of the stories herewith, and also were kind enough to share their personal notes for my reference.

Lt. General Depinder Singh PVSM AVSM
Lt. General Harwant Singh, PVSM, AVSM
Lt. General Ajai Singh, PVSM, AVSM
Air Marshal Nanda Cariappa PVSM
Air Marshal Denzil Keelor PVSM, KC, AVSM, Vir Chakra
Brigadier Surinder Singh
Brigadier Ravi Malhotra, VSM
Maj. Gen. Abdo Sandhu
Col. AS Rattan
Col. Bhupinder Singh 1 Para
Col. Sukhinder Singh 2 Sikh
Warrant Officer Brij Mohan

Abbreviations

2/Lt	2nd Lieutenant
Bn	Battalion
Brig.	Brigadier
Capt.	Captain
CAP	Combat Air Patrol
CFL	Cease Fire Line
Coy	Company
COAS	Chief of Army Staff
CRPF	Central Reserve Police Force
CO	Commanding Officer
IAF	Indian Air Force
IO	Intelligence Officer
FUP	Forming Up Place
LMG	Light Machine Gun
MAJ.	Major
MIA	Missing in Action
OG	Olive Green
OP	Operation Post
PAF	Pakistan Air Force
POA	Plan of Action
RCL	Recoilless
Sq. Ldr.	Squadron Leader
Wg. Cdr.	Wing Commander

From the Desert of Kutch …

April of Year 1965
Rann of Kutch

TURNING POINT 1

Run in the Rann

The *Rann of Kutch*—A nondescript area of salt marshes in the Thar Desert—for most Indians it is a geographic location that is usually forgotten after the school lessons are over. Sparsely inhabited with surreal landscape and a harsh terrain, it has now started getting sporadic visitors as tourists (for Ranutsav and for "Chir Batti"—the ghost lights which are an unexplained strange phenomenon of dancing lights that occur at night) but in 1965 you could barely see anyone there for miles. The northern boundary of the *Greater Rann* forms the International boundary between India and Pakistan.

As early as January of 1965, Pakistan patrol Forces started foraying into Indian territory. There was no formal border fence in those days. The Pakistan patrol even went so far as to establish a post at *Kanjarkot* in Indian territory. India lodged a formal protest, but nothing was done about it. Indian Forces stepped up patrolling, however it was of not of much use as the land was wet and marshy and restricted such activity. India's objections to Pakistan Forces patrolling the unoccupied areas on Indian side were rebuffed by Pakistan President Ayub Khan saying that the patrolling in the cited areas by Pakistani troops had always been there!

India quickly set up forward military posts during March-April 1965 as a response. No. 2 CRPF battalion established a company strength post near the border by mid-March 1965, which was named *Sardar Post*. The name had its origins in the fact that the company commander of the post was a Sikh officer, Maj Karnail Singh. A few personnel from 31 INF BDE were grouped with this force in early April, with the sole purpose of providing information of enemy activities across the border to the brigade HQ. With the arrival of the CRPF company at *Sardar Post*, preparation of defenses and patrolling activity commenced in full earnest. By April 1965, the skirmishes between the two armies started turning into small scale battles.

On April 9, 1965, at 0300 hrs, Pakistan's 51 Brigade Group, comprised of 3,500 men—commanded by Brigadier M. Azhar launched a full-scale attack on *Sardar* and *Tak* posts in *Rann of Kutch*. The attack was code-named "Operation Desert Hawk" by Pakistan Army. At the time of the attack, the border was guarded by the CRPF and Gujarat State Police Force—a total strength of hardly 150 soldiers. The Indian troops were no match for the armed enemy and the terrain was also disadvantageous for the defending forces.

At that point of time, four Coys of 2nd battalion CRPF were on duty. The Jawans fought valiantly and repulsed the attack much to the enemy's surprise during a battle that lasted almost fifteen hours. The enemy made three attempts to take complete control. The Pakistanis did succeed in overrunning the forward platoon but withdrew soon after they were thwarted on every attempt. The CRPF men used strategic thinking to stretch their limited arsenal by silencing their guns (just three machine guns, and later on one got jammed) till the enemy approached very near and then let loose a volley of shots to ensure that each bullet found a mark. Constable Shiv Ram managed to detect the enemy observation post and bravely destroyed it before the enemy could pounce on him. The CRPF company lost a few soldiers in action and a few personnel were taken prisoner by enemy forces whilst retreating, including the post commander Major Karnail Singh. The soldiers from *Tak* post had joined in to lend their support to their comrades. The enemy was forced to flee back leaving their dead behind. The CRPF troops vacated *Sardar Post* by 1530 hrs as they had run out of arsenal. The enemy shelling continued sporadically throughout the night on the post.

The DIG Police had radioed for Army's help. 2 SIKH LI was dispatched to defend the post. They arrived at *Vigokot* by 0300hrs on April 10, 1965 and immediately packed off a patrol to *Sardar Post*.

1 MAHAR was ordered to carry out the relief and occupy *Sardar Post* and this was completed by first light, April 12,1965. The enemy made a few attempts to capture the post but were beaten back every time. When the ceasefire was declared, *Sardar Post* was firmly in Indian hands.

The determination and valour of 2nd battalion CRPF Jawans kept the Pakistan Army Brigade at bay for more than fifteen hours.

This battle was a turning point for India as this repulse of the enemy intrusion did not let the enemy further into the country which would have had disastrous results for India. India realised that a special force was needed for Her borders and moved to set up a dedicated force to man the borders with Pakistan—which is how the Border Security Force (BSF) came into being. Until then India's borders with Pakistan were guarded by the State Armed Police Battalions.

The significance of this battle also lies in the morale boost to every soldier in the line of action by the sheer valour displayed by a small contingent of CRPF in repulsing a Pakistani brigade of thousands. India was a force to be reckoned with, and the enemy had taken no cognizance of the same.

Further in the area, on April 19, 1965, Pakistan's troops in the *Rann of Kutch* captured *Biar Bet* and came closer to cutting right through to the Indian Forces to destroy two Indian brigades.

On April 24, 1965, Pakistan Army cannonaded Indian posts by rolling their Patton tanks more than seven miles into the *Rann*. They found the operation relatively easy. General Ayub had chosen his battlefield strategically—the enemy troops were well serviced through better roads from the *Badin* cantonment which could replenish their supplies quickly. On the other hand, India had no roads in the *Rann* sector to support any operations. By the time Indian reinforcements could reach the units in the *Rann*, the monsoon had arrived. Further inroads by Pakistan Forces were stalled due to International pressure.

The *Rann* was a disaster in floods as not even Infantry movement was possible let alone tank movement. It was not considered prudent to launch offensive operations in this area and the Higher Commands contemplated a different front for the same. Reputed to be a strategist though overcautious, General Chaudhuri finally moved troops into Punjab—which well served a different purpose later on.

The British Prime Minister Harold Wilson finally succeeded in persuading the warring countries to end hostilities and resolve the dispute. Increasing international pressure forced Pakistan to cease fire by April 30, 1965.

The outcome of the "Operation Desert Hawk" was considered positive (for the design envisaged by Pakistan) by Field Marshal Ayub Khan. The restraint exercised by India convinced him that India was not in a fighting mood and he deduced that the stage was clear to attack India full scale.

Not obvious then, but the operations in the *Rann* were a testing ground by Pakistan to assess India's military might and, ignoring the mettle of the soldiers, they only focused on the lack of ammunition and armour and drew their own conclusions on regaling India as devoid of adequate machinery, thereby making future plans accordingly. And, in line with their future sinister plan to wrest *Kashmir*, the attacks in this terrain were also meant to divert the engagement of Indian Forces to the *Rann* sector so that the Pakistan Forces could succeed in carrying out clandestine operations to attack the main objective of *Kashmir* in subsequent months.

Notes

- This way, the BSF formally came into being on December 1, 1965.
- Pakistan would eventually get 910 square km of the Rann of Kutch against its claim of 9,100 square km.
- CRPF Valour Day is observed as "Shaurya Diwas" on April 9 every year in honour of the martyrs of this battle.

The art of war teaches us to rely not on the likelihood of the enemy's not coming, but on our own readiness to receive him; not on the chance of his not attacking, but rather on the fact that we have made our position unassailable.

—Sun Tzu

To the Mountains of Pir Panjal …

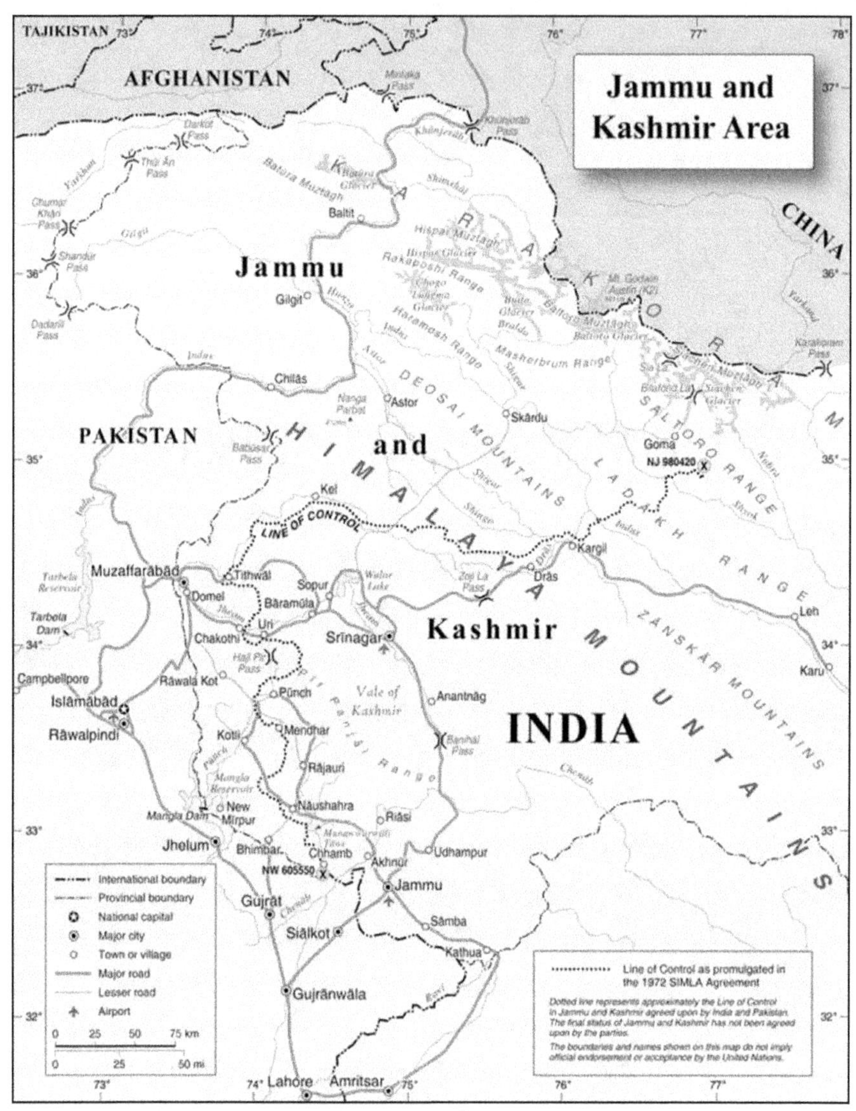

Source: http://www.indiandefencereview.com/wp-content/uploads/2015/09/Jammu-Kashmir-Map-_-UNO.jpg

May of Year 1965
Kargil Area

TURNING POINT 2

The Braveheart of Kargil

The bright sun cascading its rays over the Pir Panjal mountains and the crisp fresh air belied the danger that lurked in these ranges in the form of surreptitious activities conducted by infiltrators sneaking into Indian territory. *Kargil* is the second largest town in Ladakh after *Leh* in the Zaskar range of the Himalayas. It abuts the Line of Control between the Kashmir regions administered by India and Pakistan and remains a hotbed of activity even today.

The Indo-Pakistan War kick-started with intrusion by Pakistan Army in the *Rann of Kutch* ("Operation Dessert Hawk") under the leadership of President Ayub Khan. The Indian side did suffer a huge blow in this surprise attack. The Indian Army Chief, General J. N. Chaudhuri, advised against escalating the fight in that area as the terrain favoured Pakistan. The Indian Foreign Secretary too wanted to consider a retaliation elsewhere, where conditions would be more favourable to Indian Forces.

Beginning May 1965 Pakistan, bolstered by its success in the *Rann*, started regularly violating the ceasefire. The enemy was active in *Kargil* area and aimed to cut off the *Srinagar-Leh* highway. Pakistani infiltrators crossed the CFL and occupied three high hill features (*Tiger Hill*, *Tololing* and *Pt 4875*) and even established observation posts. As a strategic response the Indian Army planned to attack an enemy position in the *Kargil* sector. It may be noted that in May 1965 India had only one mountain division at that time. And one more division was still in the process of getting raised.

The 121 (Independent) Infantry Brigade Group in the area was tasked to capture the features known as *Point 13620* and *Black Rocks*. 4 RAJPUT being the only infantry unit available, was assigned the objective. Lt. Col. Sudarshan Singh was the CO of 4 RAJPUT and briefed his Company commanders for the operations—Maj. DP Nayyar and Maj. Randhawa who were commanding the Alpha and Bravo Coys respectively. Maj. Nayyar and his Company were assigned capture of *Black Rock* and Maj. Randhawa and his unit were tasked with the capture of *Point 13620.*

Point 13620 was well occupied by Pakistani troops, who had the vantage of observing all actions of Indian troops from that height. They were also in possession of long-range artillery fire and used it frequently to disrupt traffic on the vital *Srinagar-Kargil-Leh* road—which was the lifeline for the forward post of the Indian Army units. It was a thorn that needed to be flushed out.

Maj. Baljit Singh Randhawa was a seasoned officer who had seen action in *Gaza* and the Liberation of *Goa*. He was popular with his officers and men, an avid hockey player and at the time of the mission had just become a father for the first time to a baby boy. He and his troops barely had three days to prepare the plan to reconnoitre and capture the objective. Post preparation of the troops from May 15 to 16, the operation commenced at 1900 hrs on May 16, 1965. To ensure secrecy, local porters and ponies to carry heavy load were also ruled out.

The 'B' company was well prepared for the target to be strongly barricaded and safeguarded. The Pakistani troops had used stones and rocks to carve out bunkers which enabled them to fire at ease without exposing themselves. Surprise was a critical element in the planning of the strike by the Indian troops as they would have to reach the top of the feature undetected to minimise the time they would be directly exposed to gunfire.

The Indian troops led by Maj. Randhawa reached the FUP* around 0200 hrs on May 17—earlier than the H Hour of 0230 hrs—and they decided to press on. Since this was a silent attack, there was no War cry, only prayers on the lips and a steely resolve to get the task done—over and out. It was an arduous climb to the objective and the entire area was covered under layers of snow. There were no tracks to guide, nor any maps. The troops inched into the darkness ahead with their Commander, making their way from what was etched in their memory from the reconnaissance missions and their briefing. It was a sheer vertical climb from 10,000 ft to 14000 ft with each man carrying 20 kg of weapons and supplies—and bracing for enemy fire! Breathing in that freezing temperature and vertiginous height was also a problem, and coupled with the weight on their backs, the men were forced to go slowly.

Once they reached atop, Bravo Company immediately launched the assault with Capt. Kang leading with one platoon. The enemy (now the Northern Light Infantry) fired from their dominant post of 300 metres up on a steep slope and leveraged their position of a favourable height along with their good supply of weapons and men. It was also easy for them to spot the men in olive greens in the snow. The Indian troops did not consider stopping even once and persisted in the exhausting climb up the treacherous terrain. They not only battled the biting cold and a tempestuous wind slapping their faces but also faced a constant array of gunfire during the painstaking climb.

However, further advance of the Indian contingent was unviable due to a light machine gun post of the enemy. The Commander quickly understood that in order to proceed further and to prevent casualties mounting up, the LMG post needed to be neutralised. He did not allow himself the luxury of considering any alternatives. One look behind at the entire contingent that was his responsibility was enough for him to act. Without a thought for his own safety, Major Baljit Singh attacked the LMG post in a daredevil action—he snatched a light machine gun and surged ahead whilst simultaneously encouraging his troops to capture the enemy post. Seeing their Commander stride ahead was enough to goad the men. Well-motivated, the Bravo Company leapt forward as one force and captured the objective.

Maj. Randhawa unfortunately ended up taking a full burst of enemy fire while clearing a bunker and was gravely wounded. Despite his injury, he kept rallying his men to move forward and did not let his men attend to him even once. He later succumbed to his injuries and till today is remembered as the martyr with a rare display of courage and self-sacrifice who led gallantly from the front.

This battle was a significant turning point as it was the first time that India chose to retaliate instead of being passive and took up forward action in the face of an aggressive enemy. It was a turning point in the approach adopted by the "powers that be" in India.

This victory boosted the "esprit de corps" of the Indian Army and can be looked upon as a prelude to curb Pakistan's hostile aggression a few months down the line. Overlooking this display of courage and the offensive stance of the Indian contingent in this battle would cost the Pakistan Army dear in months to come.

The troops at the post to this date, claim that they can feel the spirit of Maj. Randhawa at the post. He apparently does not let anyone sleep on this watch!

Notes

- Maj. Baljit Singh Randhawa was awarded the "Maha Vir Chakra" posthumously for his raw courage, indomitable spirit and leadership in the line of duty.
- A Ceasefire agreement was signed on 1 July 1965. The *Kutch* issue was discussed and resolved for the moment and India withdrew from the three posts.
- The Punjab Government named a road in Amritsar in the memory of the hero, Maj. Baljit Randhawa.

Be extremely subtle, even to the point of formlessness. Be extremely mysterious, even to the point of soundlessness. Thereby you can be the director of the opponent's fate.

—Sun Tzu

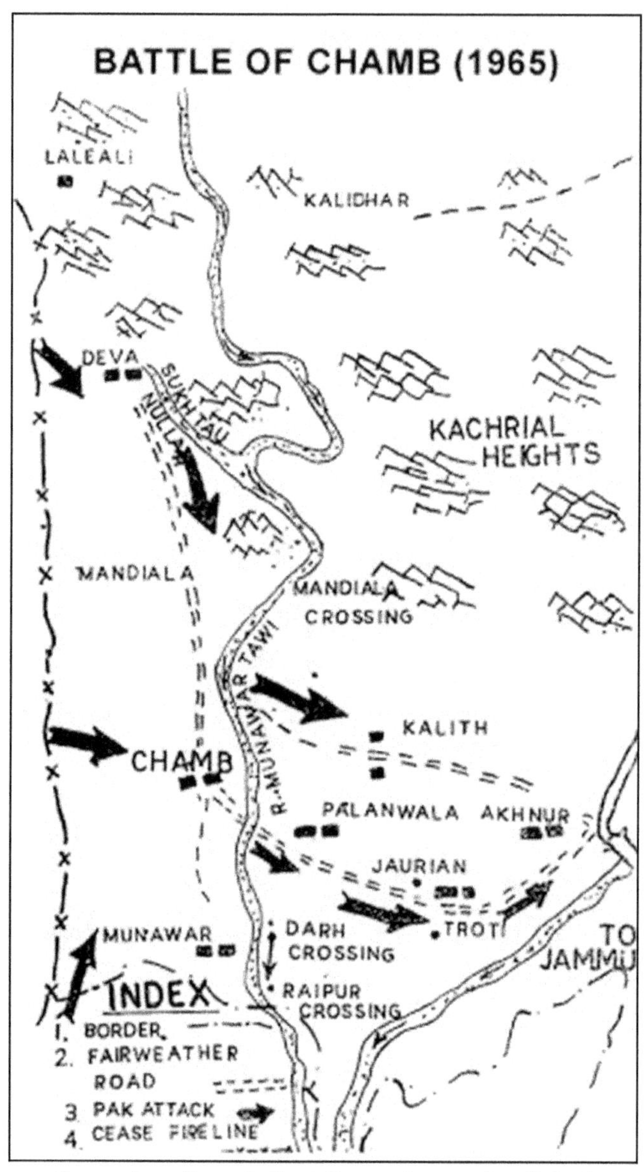

Source: http://www.indiandefencereview.com/spotlights/indo-pak-war-1965-major-actions/

August of Year 1965
Akhnoor Area

TURNING POINT 3

Courage under Fire: The Battle of Chhamb

Circa August of the Year 1965 at *Mandiala* in *Chhamb-Jourian* sector, Capt. Surinder Singh, a young officer posted as GSO3(I) in 162 Infantry Brigade was taking a round in the night amidst heavy firing going on around. He had moved along with his Commander (Brigadier Manmohan Singh) to *Mandiala* on August 16, 1965.

The sector *Chhamb-Jourian* is bound by the *Kalidhar* Range in the north and River Chenab in the south. River Manawar Tawi flowing north to south ending up in River Chenab was 6-8 km from the border (India-Pakistan CFL) and fordable by tanks in dry season. The sector is of strategic importance due to its proximity to the important Pakistani bases of *Sialkot* and *Kharian*.

The young GSO3(I) was reminiscing how just two days back on August 15, 1965, he was in the midst of his lunch at the Usman club in *Jammu* when the news of a dangerous situation built up in the *Chhamb-Jourian* sector was relayed to him by his Brigade Commander, Brigadier Manmohan Singh. On receiving orders from the Corps Commander (who was based at Udhampur), both had immediately packed up and left for *Akhnoor*, which was a good 29 km (by road) away. *Mandiala* (in *Akhnoor* area) had come under acute shelling and firing by infiltrators and both the officers were assigned to restore the situation there. They reached at nightfall and were given a brief on the prevalent chaotic situation by the Brigade Major posted there.

The young GSO3(I), all of 26 years was reflecting on the rapid turn of events in the last few days, which were unfortunately scaling up in intensity and working favourably for the Pakistani Army.

Earlier in the month, before the arrival of the young GSO3(I) in *Mandiala* 191 INF Brigade was stationed in *Akhnoor* and was responsible for the defence of the sector. There was devastating shelling and attacks in the area by infiltrators crossing the CFL and making their way into Indian territory. They aimed to detract their presence from Indian Forces with bombings and blasts in all the areas including *Mandiala*. The infiltrators were meeting resistance they were not prepared for, but they were undeterred.

The Indian soldiers, on several occasions, were at a loss to identify the infiltrators initially as they were in the garb of local citizens. The enemy artillery fire was always sudden, blistering, and volatile—it ended up scattering the Indian Forces in a disarray and more so due to lack of adequate lighting. All these activities were the strategic deployment of a wily plan by the enemy (imperceptible at that time) to let loose infiltrators in the area (trained in secrecy by the enemy) to deliberately create chaos and confusion in J&K and to inflict maximum casualties to the Indian Army stationed there. Disguised as the locals of Kashmir they sought to instigate the local Muslim population to revolt against the Indian troops. This way they aimed to assemble a local uprising which would give Pakistan Army the needed excuse to march over into India (in uniform) as a response to a claimed call for help! The saboteurs were well armed and had succeeded in spreading themselves in different organised groups in the region—this was the crux of the strategy of the operation code-named "Operation Gibraltar" of the Pakistan Army. It is estimated that around 35,000 to 45,000 infiltrators had crossed over to India.

However, this scheme of the enemy did not achieve the success they had hoped for as the local citizens of the valley not only refused to accept the infiltrators into their fold, but also alerted the Indian troops thereby helping the Indian soldiers.

Once the Indian Army sections were alerted to this activity, they swung into action to nab these infiltrators. One such operation to curb the infiltration in *Chhamb* area was planned by Brigadier Behram

Masters, Commander 191 Infantry Brigade Group. On August 14, 1965 he briefed his unit commanders about the prevailing situation and the decision to take punitive action against the infiltrators. The troops were assembled at *Mandiala*. Somehow, the enemy came to know about this design through their agents and intelligence. And, on August 15, 1965, at 0730 hrs there was a sudden violent attack on 191 Infantry Brigade causing heavy casualties and mass destruction all around. Brigadier Masters too was hit by a frontal direct fire in the line of defence whilst he was at *Dewa* post.

The Indian militia were completely bewildered seeing their Brigade Commander fall and the intensity of the fire of this surprise attack created chaos and confusion. Positions were abandoned, there was breakdown of command and there seemed to be no control over the troops. There was a cessation in communications too. Heavy crossfire continued for the next two days forcing the disarrayed Indian troops to withdraw some positions and this gave the enemy the opportunity to occupy those posts. There was a shortage of manpower, supplies and ammunition for the Indian Forces.

This chaos was the situation which greeted the young GSO3(I) and his Brigade Commander when they arrived in *Mandiala*. Immediately on arrival Brig. Manmohan Singh focused on redeploying troops to stabilise the situation and working out a plan of action. Effective measures were taken to address the chaos and panic and re-boost the morale of the troops.

By the 27th of August 1965, the situation was fully under control. Indian Infantry troops were deployed (including a squadron of tanks) ahead of *Mandiala* and the HQ relocated from *Akhnoor* to *Mandiala*. During this time Pakistan Army was also carrying out concentration of its troops.

On August 28, 1965, Capt. Surinder Singh the GSO3(I) had gone on a recce to ascertain tank presence as part of his patrolling exercise. He was wondering which of his course-mates he would be reunited with when he moved to *Miransahib* in some days. He was also planning to get married and was looking forward to living a normal life.

The breathtaking beauty of the landscape that he was admiring on that beautiful starry night was gone in the next few seconds. As he came close to the CFL he could hear some movement in the still of the night. Being an Armoured Corps officer, he could make out the subtle noise as that of Armoured tanks. He strained to see in the darkness but could not detect any silhouettes of tanks.

The tiny noise kept haunting him all the way on his return, and he decided to immediately brief his Brigade Commander and relay his fear of tank concentration being built up in the area. He reckoned at least two regiments of tanks which clearly indicated an offensive design.

The Corps Commander was meeting the Brigade Commander at *Jourian* in the morning of August 29, 1965. He was apprised of an indicative tank build-up across the CFL, but he did not take it seriously and was little perturbed. The young GSO3(I) who had accompanied his Brigade Commander was questioned sarcastically about knowing the difference between tractor noise and tank noise! When told that the young captain had 9 years of service (as opposed to 6 years of service which others holding the rank had in Infantry) and was from an Armoured Corps unit, the Corps Commander calmed down.

The Brigade Commander, though, fully trusted the GSO3(I)'s assessment and asked for additional Forces. It was already the 29th of August in 1965. The Corps Commander however went away stating he wanted troops to focus on *Haji Pir* (which had been recently captured) area and that the Brigade Commander should not panic hearing some noise!

Come September 1, 1965 Pakistan withdrew from all diplomatic talks and crossed over to Indian territory at 0500 hrs in direct violation of ceasefire—*Operation Grand Slam* was underway. They crossed from three thrust lines towards *Mandiala-Akhnoor* axis.

The "tiny" noise heard by the young GSO3(I) were "not so tiny" three coloumns of tanks—which at that time were being positioned along the ceasefire line and camouflaged well!

Field Marshal Ayub Khan of the Pakistan Army had wanted his 12 DIV to capture *Akhnoor*—so chosen because it entailed crossing a single bridge on the fast-flowing Chenab River. It was the key to

Indian communications from *Jammu* to *Rajouri-Poonch*. The bridge was also the sole all-weather lifeline of an Indian infantry division, with some 20 Infantry battalions defending *Poonch*, *Rajouri*, *Jhangar* and *Naushera*, and one independent Infantry Brigade defending *Chhamb-Dewa* sectors. Capture of *Akhnoor* would have enabled Pakistan to threaten *Jammu*, the key to all Indian communications from *Pathankot* to *Srinagar* and *Ladakh*.

Once the Pakistan Army tanks crossed over, they caused mass destruction on men and supplies as they showered constant fire along their line of advance. They had also blown up the ammunition dump at *Dewa* earlier. The Brigade Commander, Brig. Manmohan Singh asked for reinforcements again and, finally, 41 Brigade was rushed for the same and on arrival took position behind *Jourian*. Thereafter, 28 INF BDE was rushed to take position at *Fatwal* Bridge.

The Pakistan Army offensive pushed the Indian Army units to the banks of the *Munnawar Tawi* river, where a squadron of AMX 13 tanks of 20 LANCERS and elements of 6 SIKH LI Regiment and 15 KUMAON managed to bravely hold off the Pakistan Armour.

It must be noted that the enemy had a superiority in quality and quantity of Armour—in excess of 10:1. Pakistan Army was well equipped with modern Pattons—a medium tank while India possessed AMX-13-a light tank. Against the might of the two Armoured regiments (90 tanks) of the Pakistan Army equipped with the latest tanks, were just four troops of AMX-13 tanks (12 tanks) of the Indian Army!

Despite being numerically stronger, it still took Pakistani troops the better part of the day to breach the defences of 6 SIKH LI troops who were putting up a good fight along with their comrades of 20 LANCERS squadron.

15 KUMAON deployed at *Mandiala* held on as much possible and withdrew to *Jourian* only on orders after last light as unfortunately, by mid-day, their supplies had run out.

The Indian Army now anxiously requested the Indian Air Force for support to counter the desperate situation at 1000 hrs that same day, i.e.

September 1, 1965. The Indian Air Force did come but only by 1800 hrs, however they did manage to distract the enemy. Though *Chhamb* was lost that day, the combined force of the Indian Army and Air Force engagements did not let the enemy advance further and halted their ingress for that time.

At this point of time, advancing Pakistani flanks were in a position to surround the Indian contingent right away and cut them off from the rest of the country by moving towards *Akhnoor* and destroying the bridge over Chenab River. This bridge was the only link between *Poonch* valley and *Jammu* and its destruction would have enabled the Pakistan Army with a strategic position to corner the Indian troops and isolate *Jammu*. This would subsequently open the field for Pakistan to take action on *Kashmir* valley via *Poonch*. Indeed, the course of the War would have changed horrifyingly for India.

Pakistan would have been able to justify the aggression by stating that it had been necessitated by India's capture of the *Haji Pir* Pass and world opinion would largely have remained ambivalent to Pakistan—as Pakistan always maintained that they were not linked with the infiltrators and had no hand in those operations. (This stance continues to be maintained.)

However, in a strange turn of events, the Pakistan Army did not advance to *Akhnoor*. They had ample ammunition, troops and time to easily capture *Akhnoor* and destroy the bridge and could have possibly emerged victorious then and there. But they did not do that—and this pause turned the tables around.

Now unbenownest to all at that time, Pakistan Army was having a change of guard due to which the operations stalled that day and a day was lost on their count. The Corp Commander of the Pakistan Army Maj. Gen. Akhtar Hussain Malik Khan was replaced by Maj. Gen. Yahya Khan. In the absence of clear orders, the Pakistan Army did not advance further and the operation in-charge too did not use his judgement to take the logical decision.

This pause gave India just the time needed to get Her reinforcements and bolster Her defences at *Jourian* (41 Infantry Brigade could be moved up to *Jourian* quickly) and *Fatwal Ridge*—two positions which the enemy had to overcome to reach *Akhnoor*. The enemy advance was resumed only after the last light on September 3, 1965 but by then Indian Forces were replenished with men and arms to take them on. It should be noted a newly raised contingent of the Indian Army—10 Infantry Division started operations straight on this battleground!

On September 4, 1965, an unfortunate incident occurred—161 FIELD regiment at *Jourian* had abandoned their guns and had been decimated. There was strong criticism of the unit, even though the unit was ill-prepared to take on the onslaught of heavy artillery fire from the enemy without ammunitions and supplies.

Undoubtedly, Pakistan missed a golden opportunity to capture *Akhnoor*, which lay ripe for the picking. And thus "Operation Grand Slam" ground to a halt short of *Akhnoor* by September 5, 1965.

This battle was a significant turn as for the first time the Indian Army's efforts were ably supported by the IAF strikers who had pounded the Pakistan Army in a timely manner. With reinforcements and aerial cover, the troops managed to fight back valiantly and succeeded in pushing the enemy back and ensuring that "Operation Grand Slam" was slammed shut.

Notes

- The resistance put up by 191 Infantry Brigade Group had many a tale of heroism and courage of 6 SIKH LI, 15 KUMAON and 20 LANCERS (sq), which delayed the enemy on the critical first day. 3 MAHAR led by Lt. Col. Sangha also tenaciously held on to *Mandiala* Heights. The last stretch of a mere 5-7 km could not be accomplished by the enemy forces only due to the sheer grit and bold resistance of the soldiers of these units of the 191 INF BDE.
- "Operation Grand Slam" was a brilliantly conceived plan—on paper, and had all the ingredients of a successful operation. The execution was the let-down as it did not anticipate nor factor India's retaliation—which worked in India's favour.
- It was decided by the Indian Government, on the advice of the Army Chief, Gen. J. N. Chaudhuri to open another front across the International border in a different terrain—to relieve the pressure in J&K where the situation was getting uncomfortable for the Indian Army. Therefore "Operation Riddle" was launched on September 6, 1965 by the Indian Army and this succeeded in stabilising the situation in *Akhnoor*. The Pakistan Army had lost the initiative in *Chhamb* when the Indian Army decided to cross the International Boundary near *Lahore* to take the War right to Pakistan's

doorstep in the coming days. With this launch of operations by India on September 6, Pakistan was forced to pull back the major component of its offensive forces from the *Chhamb* Sector and a stalemate developed in the Chhamb sector which was to continue till the declaration of the ceasefire.

- It may be noted here that Pakistan contingent in the sector included a newly raised 6 Armoured Division which the Indian side had NO knowledge of—the intelligence inputs of India were sadly lacking.
- Maj. Bhaskar Rai of 20 LANCERS was awarded an MVC.

The opportunity to secure ourselves against defeat lies in our own hands, but the opportunity of defeating the enemy is provided by the enemy himself.

—Sun Tzu, *The Art of War*

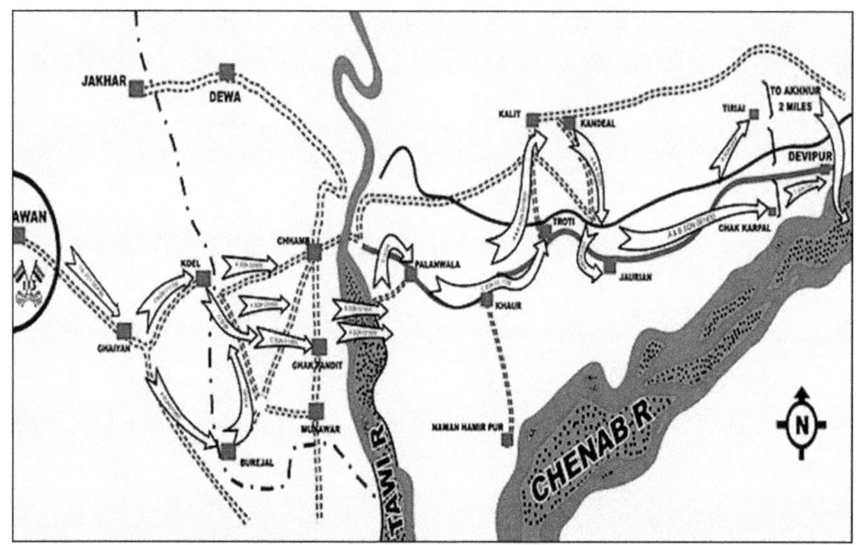

Source: https://mashalbutt.wixsite.com/13lancersspearheads/battle-of-akhnur-65

August of Year 1965
Chhamb Sector

TURNING POINT 4

The Warrior of Mandiala Heights

In August of 1965, when Pakistan launched "Operation Gibraltar" several columns of infiltrators were dispatched into India. When the Indian troops became aware and took countermeasures, the enemy launched its offensive with even more ferocity.

On August 15, 1965, the infiltrators conducted a surprise attack on *Dewa* camp in J&K. The Indian troops came under massive concentrated artillery fire from the enemy and the Brigade Commander, Brigadier Masters was killed. At that time, 3 MAHAR was in the process of hand-over to 2 SIKH when they were rushed to *Dewa-Chhamb* sector—unfortunately, without their heavy weapons, since those had been handed over. (It is believed that the troops were watching a movie in the unit hall while waiting for their transport to the next post when the message came on the screen asking them to report immediately to command station!)

Lieutenant Colonel Gurbans Singh Sangha was commanding the battalion of 3 MAHAR. He hailed from a family of long military tradition and was a seasoned leader. At the battle site he inspired his men to repulse the continuous downpour of enemy fire with the little ammunition they had. Unfortunately, their communications were lost due to a temporary breakdown and the Brigade headquarters had no idea of their whereabouts. They were literally on their own! The men continued the vigil bravely, despite heavy enemy shelling, inspired by their CO.

Lt. Col. Sangha used his astute judgement and deployed his men at a feature called *Mandiala Heights* (the elevated ground to the north of Mandiala crossing—where the road from Chhamb crosses Munnawar wali Tawi). This quick-thinking and sensible act gave the troops a better control over the situation, and the motivation to achieve the objective of stalling the advance of the enemy.

Despite being disconnected, the battalion carried on their operations. They foiled the attempts of the infiltrators occupying strongholds in Indian and who were expecting an easy passage to reach *Jourian* and did not let any of the infiltrators pass through. On August 17, 1965 'B' Company of the regiment was dispatched to clear the enemy at *Maira* and accomplished their mission. 'C' Company personally led by Lt. Col. Sangha attacked *Nathuan Tiba* in a daring bayonet charge and managed to evict the enemy. They zealously guarded these posts and prevented any further ingress of the enemy. These were extremely extenuating circumstances and the men went without food for several days.

On September 1, 1965, Pakistan trespassed with full armour into Indian territory under "Operation Grand Slam." For an infantry unit to combat a tank attack whilst holding ground is absolutely unthinkable. A tank is a moving loaded bomb on the move, but it cannot climb hills. Lt. Col. Sangha had cleverly extricated his troops to *Mandiala Heights* and moved them to a terrain where the tanks could not reach. It was a precarious situation still as the battalion had no munitions except some machine guns and rifles, which were no match for the armour of the tanks or the guns, let alone constitute a deterrent. The absence of the anti-tank weapons was acutely felt by the entire team of the battalion that day.

3 MAHAR was physically severed from the other units, though voice communication was established for a short while. The enemy tanks too started encircling them soon. Lt. Col. Sangha spoke to Brigade HQ and was assured that artillery and air support would come and told to continue holding the post. Unfortunately, none of the promised support came but the heroism of the troops is legendary as they managed to hold off against all odds by being constantly rallied by their CO.

By nightfall, the entire brigade had orders to pull back behind *Munawar Tawi* River except 3 MAHAR and 9 PUNJAB as both had to continue to hold their respective positions to delay the enemy advance.

An isolated army can usually never get the motivation to continue the vigil specially when surrounded from all sides by the enemy. It is psychologically damaging and fearful. Lt. Col. Sangha ensured his men did not go through any of that. This is where the leadership of a commanding officer comes in. He shored up and roused his men like none other and did not let fear or panic set in. He lived up to their trust in him by being constantly by the side of his men.

Lalialli post, defended by a squadron post of 3 MAHAR was the first to come under direct enemy fire. The CO advised his men to strategically wait until the enemy was 250 yards away before opening fire so that they could conserve their limited arsenal and score maximum hits. This act wreaked havoc on the enemy troops as they were expecting to capture the Indian troops, and they dispersed in confusion. But at nightfall the post came under another attack—fierce and threatening.

Now the entire 3 MAHAR contingent was devoid of any ammunition and none of the reinforcements could reach them. It was not prudent to continue a defence in these circumstances, so they withdrew to form part of the defence box of the entire battalion. The valiant soldiers continued to repulse enemy efforts to dislodge them but were on the receiving end of a constant barrage of gunfire.

Communications with the Brigade were re-established on September 4 and on September 6, Lt. Col. Sangha received the news of the offensive in the Punjab Theatre. And, as predicted, the Pakistan Forces were forced to withdraw from *Chhamb* to counter the Indian threat on another battleground.

This was a critical turning point in the War as 3 MAHAR, led dauntlessly by their CO, did not let the enemy inch into Indian territory on their beat. Had they succumbed to the psychological and pressure tactics of the enemy India's map would be having a different design altogether.

Note

- Lt. Col. Sangha was decorated with Mahavir Chakra for his outstanding leadership in the Battle.

In war there is no prize for runner-up.

—Lucius Annaeus Seneca.

August of Year 1965
Poonch Area

TURNING POINT 5

The Topa Fray

In August 1965, several columns of Pakistani Army were dispatched into India as infiltrators under Pakistan's "Operation Gibraltar." Indian Intelligence had reports of major infiltration in *Mendhar* and *Balnoi* and some of the roads had been blocked by the Pakistani troops. Closer to *Mendhar*, Pakistan Army had occupied *Topa* feature, which effectively dominated the road *Mendhar-Balnoi*, thus cutting off Balnoi and *Krishna Ghati* and the Indian batallions thereof (93 Infantry Brigade).

Topa (point 4571) is a village in *Mendhar* Tehsil in *Poonch* district in Jammu and Kashmir. In addition to *Topa* feature, the infiltrators had also established defences at a place called *OP Hill*, on the ridgeline across *Mendhar* River. The priority of the Indian Army was to cut off supply routes of the enemy troops and then tackle the clearance of *Balnoi-Krishna Ghati* road. Alpha Company of 21 AK Battalion of Pakistan Army were reported to be occupying *Topa* feature.

Topa feature consisted of three hubs: *Point 4571* (Topa Top); *Gujar Kotha*, feature on its southern slopes; and a Ring Contour further to the south, called *Jungle Tekri* overlooking the road. The Indian Brigade decided to launch a deliberate attack to capture these positions and open the road up to prevent further foray into India, as well as to restore communications with the other Indian units which were cut off. The task of capturing *Topa* was given to 4/5 GORKHA RIFLES.

The Gorkhas are known for their legendary bravery. Their swift action, coupled with their prowess with the "Khukri" and accompanied by the blood curling War cry "Ayo Gorkhali" make them a force not to be messed with. The battalion concentrated on August 25, 1965 at *Mendhar* for commencement of its operations.

On August 26, 1965, the Indian troops came under assault fire from *Jungle Tekri* and *Gujar Kotha*. They launched operations the same day and the area of *Jungle Tekri* was captured by 'B' Coy led by Major Sunit Singh. It turned out this post was being used as a forward element of *Topa* defences by the enemy.

It was then decided to launch a deliberate attack the next day, i.e., August 27, to capture the main feature. The task of capture of *Topa Top* was given to Delta Company led by Capt. Bikram Katoch, Bravo Company led by Maj. Sunit Singh and Charlie Company led by Maj. Ashok Mehta, as firm base and reserve company respectively. Colonel Bhatia, the Commanding Officer did not restrict himself to only giving briefing orders for the attack but was out with his troops along with the leading Company, just behind the leading Platoon.

Come August 27, 1965, Capt. Bikram Katoch led the assault of his company. His CO, Lt. Col. M. L. Bhatia, followed the leading platoon of D Company. As soon as the troops reached closer to the objective *Gujar Kotha (*position below Pt 4571-*Topa Top*), they came under a discharge of enemy fire. They unsheathed their "Khukris" and bellowing their War cry of "Ayo Gorkhali" assaulted the position directly in complete daredevilry. Despite the barrage of constant gunfire, the GORKHAS refused to back down and by afternoon of the day the area of *Gujar Kotha* was captured.

Although the defences had been captured Pt 4571 was still held in enemy hands. Now, D Company pressed on relentlessly and by evening *Topa Top* was in their hands.

This was a critical turning point as, once the Topa sector was secured in Indian hands, there were no further infiltrators from this feature and road communication was opened up to the stranded units. Had this not been done, the enemy would have control over the estranged troops as well as an easy ingress into Indian space.

> *Victory usually goes to the army who has better trained officers and men.*
>
> —Sun Tzu

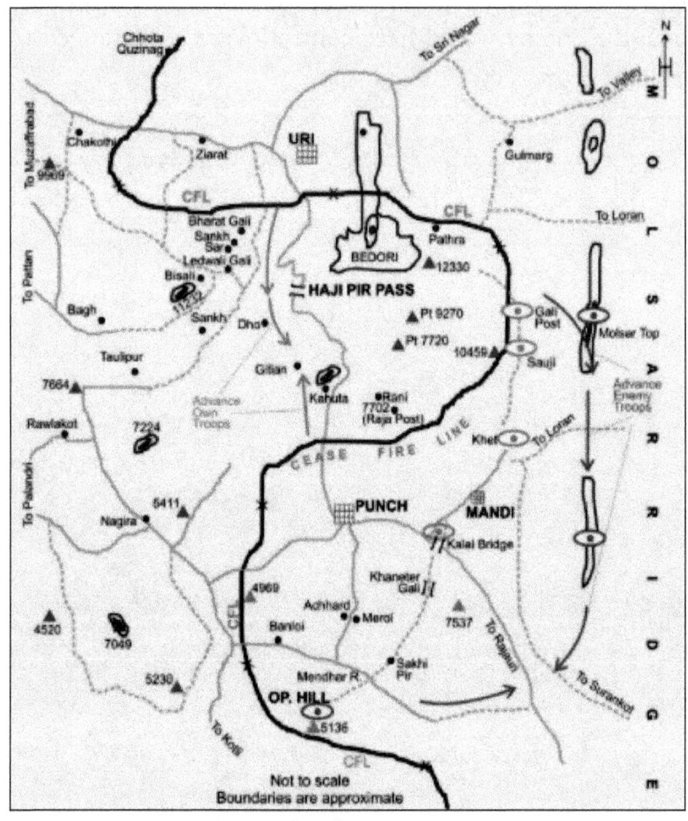

Source: https://soldier2ndlife.com/card/hajipir-captured-on-ground,
-lost-on-the-table

August of Year 1965
Pir Panjal Range

TURNING POINT 6

The Conqueror of Haji Pir

In August 1965, once Indian Forces had defended their positions and territories post the launch (and subsequent failure) of "Operation Gibraltar" they leveraged that success to carry out offensive operations—the first one being to capture the crucial *Haji Pir* (*Point 13620* in military parlance). The *Haji Pir Pass* stands tall at 8,652 feet and lies in the *Pir Panjal* range and is the highest access point connecting *Uri* to *Poonch* in the Kashmir valley. The Higher Commands in India agreed that just defending their territory was not enough, and a bold stance was needed to go across the border and plug in the major routes for infiltrators to India.

Offensive plans in *Kargil*, *Tithwal* and *Uri-Poonch* (*Haji Pir Bulge*) sectors were under way soon. The plan for capture of *Haji Pir*—the most formidable and the most critical post was put in place as early as August 15, 1965.

Haji Pir—the prized bastion of the Pakistani Forces—was zealously guarded and was being used to inflict maximum damage to India since it was snatched from India in the 1948 War. It was a stronghold for the Pakistani Forces in 1965 and it was considered unthinkable for anyone from the Indian side to even consider going near the area let alone dream of capturing it without getting annihilated. *Haji Pir's* location commanded strategic importance for the Pakistan Army to penetrate into India—this bit of land protruding into Indian territory is called the "Chicken's Neck." The pass was dominated by three neighbouring hill features: on the east by *Bedori* (3,760 m height); on the west by *Sank* (2,895 m); and on the south-west by *Ledwali Gali* (3,140 m). It was critical to capture these posts in order to reach *Haji Pir Pass* (2,637 m). *Bedori* was 14 km away from the CFL and *Haji Pir Pass* was 10 km south-west of *Bedori*—which meant that the enemy would have to be pushed off the heights on either side—a daunting task indeed!

The operational strategy comprised "Operation Faulad"—to clear the approaches to *Haji Pir* and "Operation Bakshi" (named after Brig. Bakshi who was leading the operations) which was the final operation, i.e. the assault on *Haji Pir*. This was planned to be a two-pronged simultaneous offensive—a north side attack by 68 INF Brigade (as part of 19 INF DIV) led by Brigadier Zoru Bakshi himself and the south side attack by 93 INF Brigade (under 25 INF DIV). A frontal attack was ruled out as it would have been too risky and would have exposed the Indian team to direct enemy fire.

Brig. Bakshi was a source of inspiration for the men on the field. He was a living legend—an experienced Commander who had overseen operations in *Congo* and in the 1947-48 War too. He had done military reconnaissance of areas (400 km on foot) in the guise of a Tibetan monk for 80 days in 1949. He was known for his planning and tactical skills along with great leadership and sharing the hardships of the troops.

Since the *Haji Pir* bulge was well manned by Pakistan Army units and had good artillery support cover, it was therefore essential for Indian troops to create diversionary attacks around so that the enemy did not get an inkling of the actual operations on *Hajipir*. Secrecy was the name of the game in order to achieve success on the mission.

The D-day was initially fixed as August 25, 1965 and H hour was 2200 hrs.

Operation Bakshi: Fine-tuned by the Brigadier himself, the plan was crisp and called for precision timing and efficiency in stealth approach to achieve the objective. It comprised:

Western approach (Uri-Sank) where:

1 PARA was to capture *Sank* and *Lediwali Gali* by 0500 hrs on D-day + 1

4 RAJPUT was to pass through 1 PARA and capture Haji Pir Pass by 1800 hrs D-Day+1

Eastern approach (Uri-Bedori) was assigned to 19 PUNJAB who was tasked with taking Bedori by D-Day + 1 and other assignments.

The operation start was delayed by 24 hrs due to bad weather—torrential rains, slippery ground and overflowing rivers inhibited any movement. However, despite the weather not clearing up the next day too, the Indian team decided to carry out the plan. The operation finally commenced at 2150 hrs on August 25, 1965 led by Maj. Ranjit Singh Dayal. Major Dayal was also a seasoned officer. His nascent induction in the Army had him participating in the 1947-48 War straightaway. He had also served with the UN emergency force at *Gaza.*

1 PARA initiated the operations with an attack on *Sank* Ridge reaching the base of *Sank.* The approach to the ridge was exceedingly difficult and compounded by the incessant cloudbursts of the previous night, had made the ground treacherously perilous. The progress became extremely slow because of which the attack got daylighted. *Sank* was also a well-fortified feature. The enemy cleverly held fire till the leading troops reached within 45 meters of the perimeter fencing and then opened with a blast of gunfire. This did not deter the troops of 1 PARA and the battle continued close to the fenced trenches of the enemy till 0930 hrs when the effort had to be called off. Maj. Dayal himself carried some injured soldiers down the slope to safety.

The second attack by 1 PARA commenced at 2230 hrs that night on August 26, 1965. 'B' Company led by Maj. Ranjit Singh Dayal (2IC) charged up the slopes of *Sank* supported by artillery cover fire this time. And this time 1 PARA Forces went in smaller groups. They were determined to get to the objective that night. The rain splattered grime on their faces, visibility was extremely poor, and though they were mostly wading in slush their spirits were still high. The troops clambered 800 steep vertical meters with a deafening wind in their ears and relentless beating rain which kept halting their progress. Most of the time they had no choice but to move forward on all fours!

By 0430 hrs on August 27, the Indian troops had reached within 450 meters of the enemy positions, where they formed up and in a reckless action charged frontally—not wanting to take any more time by looking for a less exposed route! Once 1 PARA announced themselves with grenades and bullets, the enemy troops rushed forward from their trenches and opened fire quickly, but this time the fierce fire from the Indian artillery forced them to crawl back to their trenches. The enemy withdrew to *Sar* and *Ledwali Gali* in the heat of this onslaught.

Fuelled by victory over *Sank*, Maj. Arvinder Singh and his Company rushed to *Sar*. They captured *Sar* too and advanced upon *Ledwali Gali* as there was machine gun fire emanating from there on the Indian troops. The enemy did put up a strong resistance but then wisely withdrew their troops from surrounding areas by 1100 hrs.

'B' Company meanwhile had secured the features around the pass—*Sawan Pathri* and *Agiwas* by 1400 hrs in the face of minor opposition from the enemy. 'C' Company had reached *Sank* and was ordered to clear the area south of Sank including *Point 10033*, which it successfully did by last light. 1 PARA achieved all the objectives assigned to it. Now 4 RAJPUT was awaited to go through for the final assault. Unfortunately, 19 PUNJAB operations were held up and they could not capture *Bedori* by the allotted time.

At this point, the troops of 1 PARA had been fighting non-stop for 48 hrs and that too after an exhausting march to reach the battleground! However, they had come near the foot of the pass and did not want to stop—the "josh" was running very high! They were exhausted in body but not in spirit!

It may be noted here that Brig. Bakshi had been wrongly conveyed that *Bedori* had been already captured, and, therefore asked 4 RAJPUT to occupy *Bedori*. And 4 RAJPUT were very surprised to come under attack when they advanced on the evening of August 26 as it was supposed to be devoid of Pakistani troops. Their request for artillery fire was not entertained and 4 RAJPUT was stalled at the base of *Bedori* because of this miscommunication.

Since the progress along the right prong had not kept pace with the left prong, CO 1 PARA (Lt. Col. Prabhjinder Singh) requested the Brigade Commander (Brig. Bakshi) for orders to go for *Haji Pir Pass*. Brig. Bakshi was also pressed for time. With the right flank of the Pass still not secured, and aware that by now Pakistan Forces would have guessed what the Indian troops were trying to capture (Pakistan Army had already rushed 18 PUNJAB on the night of August 27 as reinforcement to *Haji Pir*) it was vital to press on. And the only bleak chance of success to capture *Haji Pir* Pass now lay in a frontal attack. The risk was that the advance would be under observation of the enemy but Brig. Bakshi gave the green signal to 1 PARA.

On the final front at *Haji Pir*, Maj. Dayal and his men scaled the elevation by night carrying heavy loads, and even wading through knee-deep water which was icy cold. The troops starting from *Ledwali Gali* planned to infiltrate through *Hyderabad Nullah* on night of August 27 and capture *Ring Contours* 1194 and 1094 to proceed further. The troops had been in continuous operations for over two days and all further moves were in incessant rainstorms, sludge, hazy visibility and under artillery bombardment. Their meals consisted of crumbly biscuits and hardened shakarparas! Now, they had been on the move for three continuous nights and without sleep. But the enthusiasm of Maj. Dayal to achieve the objective marshalled the Forces, boosted their morale and filled them with confidence. They battled the cumbersome rain and the slime and focused on attaining their goal with a single-minded purpose.

By 0600 hrs they reached the base of the pass and came immediately under a hail of enemy gunfire. The team strategically split into two at this point, and Maj. Dayal with one batch scaled the western shoulder of the pass (an arduous climb of 1,220 metres) whilst the other comrades engaged the enemy in a crossfire and diverted their attention. Maj. Dayal then unbelievably simply rolled down on the enemy from his side—completely baffling the enemy in a bold daylight attack! The enemy was completely bewildered and abandoned their weapons in confusion and fled the scene. At 1030 hrs on August 28, 1965, 1 PARA was the proud occupier of *Haji Pir*—the toughest frontier and the Indian flag was unfurled there. The unimaginable had been achieved! The whole country was euphoric, and the news was even aired on Air India Radio.

However, 1 PARA had no time to celebrate as they were aware that the enemy would be seething at this conquest. They set about preparing for the counterattack intelligently, and requested for reinforcements to prepare adequately.

The enemy did try a counter-strike on August 29, 1965 to regain their post but were repulsed by the Indian Force whose adrenaline was still running high and who successfully kept them at bay for two more days.

This remarkable achievement was possible because of excellent leadership, the element of surprise and ability of the battalion to quickly regroup and continue attacking without giving the enemy time to re-organise. The daring tactics despite the antagonistic weather and inhospitable terrain turned the chin up of the Indian Army. The mindset of the commander to seize an opportunity and give it impetus with speed of action without giving any chance to the enemy to realign its forces has become a legend in War chronicles.

On August 31, 1965, the 1 PARA soldiers had their first good meal thanks to the air dropping of "aloo-puri" kindly organised by Flt. Lt. LK Dutta (father of actress Lara Dutta). He was Maj. Arvinder Singh's course-mate and had got to know that the troops had not had food since August 25, so he made arrangements for the brave warriors.

Consequently, 1 PARA pressed on and captured more areas including *NR 1092* and *Point 8786*. Eventually, 19 PUNJAB linked up on September 1, 1965 with 1 PARA and the indestructible *Haji Pir* bulge was sealed. The unthinkable had been done and the unconquerable had been surmounted!

Notes

- This was India's first official surgical strike.
- On August 16, 1965, about one lakh Indian citizens had converged in a procession and marched towards Parliament demanding that India take strong action against Pakistan. Perhaps due to public pressure Prime Minister Lal Bahadur Shastri took the bold decision of directing troops to cross the border.

- The leadership exhibited by Brig. Bakshi and Maj. Dayal is noteworthy and was solely responsible for galvanising the troops and building their determination and, most importantly, leading by example. In a War this can make or break the momentum required.
- Unfortunately, *Haji Pir* was handed back to Pakistan after the Tashkent agreement much to the chagrin of the Indian Army. It remains a point of infiltration for terrorists into Indian territory.
- Maj. Ranjit Singh Dayal, awarded the Maha Vir Chakra in 1965, said in an interview during 2002, "The Pass would have given India a definite strategic advantage.... It was a mistake to hand it back ... our people don't read maps."
- 1 PARA was awarded the "Battle Honor Haji Pir."
- Brig. Z. Bakshi was decorated with the Maha Vir Chakra. He was already a recipient of the Vir Chakra for action in the 1947-48 War. He also earned a PVSM 6 years later in action in 1971. He had earned a VSM for operations in Congo.
- Despite being a Sikh officer, Lt. Gen. Dayal was made in charge of "Operation Blue Star" by Mrs. Gandhi in 1984. He did his duty to the fullest but was ostracised by SGPC.
- I PARA is now Special Forces and continues to hold an elite and esteemed position within the Indian Army having achieved many successes in various missions.

The General who wins the battle makes many calculations in his temple before the battle is fought. The General who loses makes but few calculations beforehand.

—Sun Tzu

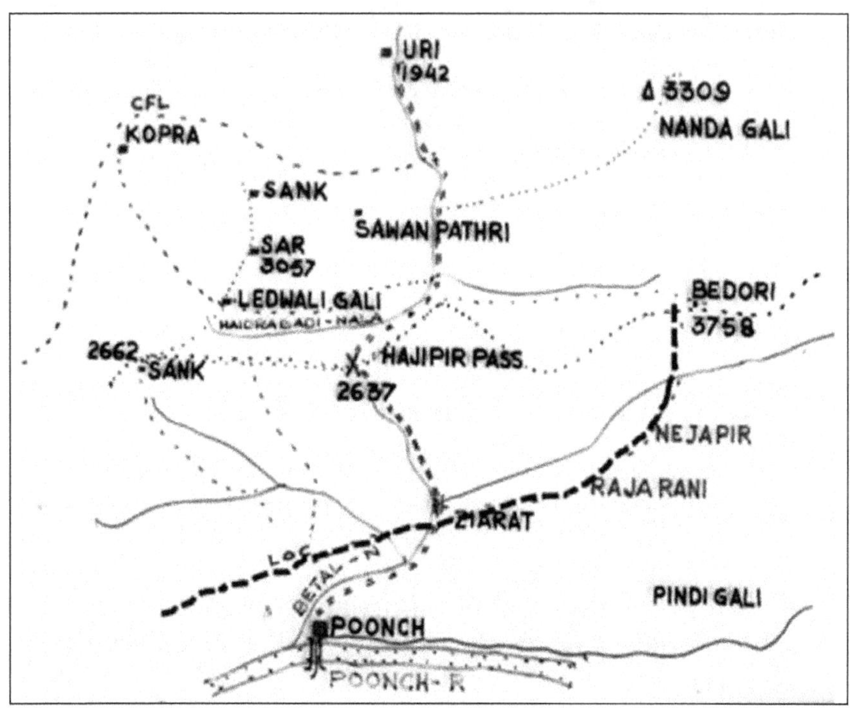

Source: https://idsa.in/system/files/jds/jds_9_3_2015_BattleofHajiPir_0.pdf

August of Year 1965
Pir Panjal Range

TURNING POINT 7

The Victors of Bedori

Once Haji Pir was selected for capture by Indian troops, the assigned units swung into action.

The Western approach operations achieved success as planned. The other side was the *Eastern approach* (Uri-Bedori) as under:

> 19 PUNJAB to capture *Ring Contour*, *Pathra* and *Point 12330* (Bedori feature) by 0100 hours D-day plus 1.
> 19 PUNJAB to capture *Bedori* and *Kuthnar di Gali* by 0600 hrs D-Day plus 1.
> 19 PUNJAB was to exploit up to *Point 11107* and establish contact with 1 PARA by 1800 hours on D+1.

19 PUNJAB under Col. Sampuran Singh also launched operations on August 25, 1965. They had reached FAA after a 30-mile march from *Uri.* The rampant rain, the dampness and the sodden terrain made the wait a sheer torture, but the PUNJABIS waited for the signal to forge ahead—and come it did at 1400 hours on the 25th of August. Despite the deluge, the PUNJABIS pressed on. They were soaked through with incessant downpour and weighed down with supplies and ammunition, but they trudged on through the slush. They were held up by the tributary of the *Haji Pir* Nullah (Hathlanga nullah), which was overflowing with the torrential rain. They still decided to carry forth though in crossing the fast-flowing waters, three men were unfortunately swept away.

The PUNJABIS secured their first FUP short of ring contour (*Point 8336)*, by midnight and, in a bold move, had their first objective by 0200 hrs. The distance to the next objective (*Bedori*) being 2,000 yards, the battalion moved forward to the second FUP, short of *Bedori* at 0300 hrs and reached it by 0345 hrs. At precisely 0400 hrs, immediately on crossing the start line, they came under heavy machine-gun fire from the enemy post. The cliffs with steep precipices and the thundering rainstorm made it difficult for the brave warriors to continue the attack especially when the Pakistani Forces were showering bullets from the comfort of their stone bunkers directly on them.

Bedori was the locus of a platoon of 6 AZAD KASHMIR of Pakistan Army. Warned by the attacks on *Sank* by 1 PARA and the PUNJAB regiment, they were well prepared for the Indian armament. The enemy was established in well-fortified bunkers which had a single approach along a razor-sharp ridge, and that too was heavily mined and covered by machine-gun fire on fixed lines. They comfortably stopped each attempt to assault them right in its tracks. Finally, not seeing any window of opportunity the CO, Lt. Col. Sampuran Singh, consulted the Brigade Commander and called off the attack at 1000 hrs and the battalion returned to *Uri.*

4 RAJPUT were ordered to attack *Bedori* that night (August 26) itself. The RAJPUTS ran into the same staunch defence as their predecessors for *Bedori.* It was impossible to deploy more than a single section along the line of the thin razor ridge, and the RAJPUT's CO, Lieutenant Colonel Sudarshan Singh, soon realised that with more and more casualties coming in, it was not going to be possible to break the enemy's defence. The attack was called off with great reluctance. This was the second setback in two nights. *Bedori* had to be cleared and was a big obstacle and so on the third night, August 28, 1965, 7 BIHAR took up the offensive, but they too were pushed back.

Meanwhile, Colonel Sampuran Singh had asked the Brigade HQ on August 28, 1965 to task his unit with the capture *Bedori* again as he wanted to try a different approach—from the east this time. The Brigadier agreed and the Punjabis duly swivelled east on the night of August 28, 1965. 19 PUNJAB soldiers had been on the move since August 25, carrying weighty ammunition and supplies in the frigid cold and ceaseless rain. Their food had run out and there was nothing growing in the heights that they were at. An attempted airdrop of food was organised but that was unfortunately swept away with the wind and the rain, much to the chagrin of the soldiers.

Though the soldiers were fatigued and tired, they were still determined to win the objective. They moved with resolve on August 29 on receiving the orders for another attack on *Bedori*. They were well charged up by their CO. 19 PUNJAB now crossed the ceasefire line near *Gagarhil* and moving up the *Dothalian Nullah* to *Bedori Springs* (11,500 ft). This approach was terribly narrow. It was a two-phased attack with Bravo Company taking the lead. They managed to climb up the *Bedori* spur undetected—and then it was a merciless fight. Charlie Company following close behind rushed in to support the assault and the gruesome feud continued. By 0600 hrs on August 29, 1965 *Bedori* feature was in Indian hands! The PUNJABIS had traversed 40 km by foot and 20 km by vehicles in an unbelievable time of 24 hours wherein they scaled a height of 10,000 ft (*Pathra*), came down to 4,000 ft (*Uri*), and were again climbing to 11,000 ft and then on to 12000 ft—without taking a break and with an agonisingly heavy load on their backs.

After a few hours rest, but still without food, the dauntless and resolute PUNJABIS carried on to their next objective and took *Kuthnar Di Gali* by the morning of August 30, 1965. They reached the *Haji Pir* Pass on the morning of September 1, 1965 and established the link-up with 1 PARA. Thus concluded "Operation Bakshi" successfully.

And finally, on September 1, 1965 the battle weary but fired up men of 19 PUNJAB finally got to eat a proper meal other than the crumbly biscuits that they had been sustaining on.

Notes

- Lt. Col. Sampuran Singh was decorated with a Maha Vir Chakra and the Vir Chakra for this operation.
- The unit was given the Battle Honour Bedori and the Theatre Honour Haji Pir.

Regard your soldiers as your children, and they will follow you into the deepest valleys; look on them as your own beloved sons, and they will stand by you even unto death.

—Sun Tzu

August of Year 1965
Poonch Area

TURNING POINT 8

Crowning the Ring

The undulating landscape of the mountains in *Poonch* was a sight for sore eyes, but to the men of 1 PARA of the Indian Army it concealed hidden dangers. The Indian troops who had emerged victors of the conquest of the *Haji Pir* pass had no time for a proper meal, let alone a celebration. The nation, though, well celebrated the glory of that victory and broadcast it well. The Indian Forces wanted to achieve the full objective of not just rounding up the enemy infiltrators who were wreaking havoc in J&K along with ambushing the army contingents but also wanted to seal off all ingress points for the enemy.

Once the Indian Army had captured *Haji Pir* with *Bedori* feature, they turned their attention to the *Ring Contour* which was harbouring an enemy build-up. *Ring Contour* was around 1,500 metres south west of the *Haji Pir* pass and the enemy had started bombardment from there. By morning of August 30, 1965 the explosions from *Ring Contour* became intense. I PARA Delta Company under Major Arvinder Singh was ordered to capture the area.

Delta Company troops made swift preparations. Maj. Arvinder Singh left at 04300 hrs on August 30 with 2 platoons to recce and ascertain the strength of the enemy contingent. It was another steep chase. The last 100 ft of the climb was particularly arduous and exhausting. Once there, Maj. Arvinder Singh observed that the enemy had already built trenches and were in considerable large numbers—and sooner than later would attack

Haji Pir anytime. Being at a propitious height the enemy had a good advantage and would be in a position to succeed in their objective. Now Maj. Arvinder Singh hardly had a second to decide whether to attack then and there or withdraw (which would give the enemy good time). He decided to take a chance and audaciously went for the kill rightaway!

Shouting their Ahir War cry "Kishan Maharaj Ki Jai" Maj. Singh and his handful of men charged brazenly at the enemy. It must be noted here that the men were already in the fifth day of continuous operations, their batteries were not charged and they had no communications lines especially since they were supposed to be on a recce, not attack, mission.

Though the enemy was taken by surprise, they repulsed the attack comfortably and were well stocked with ammunition. Soon enough it became a bloody confrontation. Grenades whizzed at each other, guns were fired at close range and the Earth was rapidly soaked in rivulets of blood. It was ferocious, it was vicious, it was frightful—the Indian troops fought tooth and nail down to hand-to-hand combat. Maj. Arvinder Singh too was wounded with a mortar shrapnel slicing through his calf. He could barely walk but he still kept the enemy at bay using his gun.

Meanwhile at *Haji Pir*, Maj. Dayal hearing the gun shots correctly understood that the recce team could be having a situation. He quickly dashed to their aid with his reserve of men and had the foresight to request for further reinforcements. He reached in an hour and a half and found Maj. Singh lying with his leg nearly blown off and still putting up a fight with only his gun. Maj. Dayal quickly jumped into the fray. It was broad daylight and the enemy brought down all the firepower at their disposal. The battle raged all day wherein the brave Delta troopers fought with all they had to push the enemy back. They lost many of their comrades—and that only served to egg them on to avenge their brothers. Reinforcements reached by evening and the post was finally taken.

The bravery exhibited by Lance Naik Jai Singh is commendable. He was standing next to Maj. Dayal and got hit in the leg. Despite bleeding profusely, he continued transmitting grid references to the Artillery team, as directed by Maj. Dayal. Thus, nine people beat back the enemy till reinforcements came and saved the day.

The next morning makeshift stretchers were designed (tying sheets between two poles) to evacuate the injured who were in pain and agony. There was no morphine available to help bear the pain and the men really suffered. They solicited the help of the local people to carry the injured men. The villagers of *Uri* area were simple folk and also very poor. They were offered double the rate of porters to carry the injured troops—that money would have meant a lot to them as they were living in extreme poverty. Much to the sheer astonishment of Maj. Singh and the men of 1 PARA these villagers refused to accept the money for carrying down the wounded. It was their contribution to Mother India and their respect for the Indian Army.

The sealing of the Ring contour completed the turnaround commenced with the capture of Haji Pir. It gave an immense boost to the morale of the Indian Forces.

Notes

- Maj. Arvinder Singh was evacuated to Army Base Hospital Srinagar and then to Agra and he lived to tell the tale.
- This feature too was given back to Pakistan after the Tashkent declaration—which brought tears to the eyes of many a soldier who had seen their comrades dying in this barbaric battle.

Be extremely subtle, even to the point of formlessness. Be extremely mysterious, even to the point of soundlessness. Thereby you can be the director of the opponent's fate.

—Sun Tzu

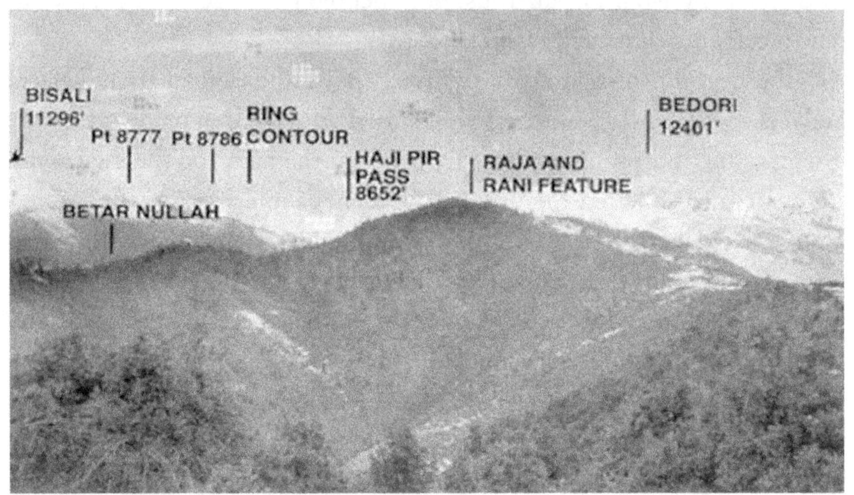

Source: http://www.indiandefencereview.com/news/fifty-years-since-haji-pir-where-did-we-go-wrong/

August of Year 1965
Pir Panjal sector

TURNING POINT 9

The King of Kings

As dusk settled in on August 28, 1965, and the Indian Army commanders had indulged in the rare luxury of a toast to the capture of *Haji Pir* pass, thoughts turned to the other daunting tasks that lay ahead for the security of the nation. The infiltration routes still needed to be plugged. The focus of efforts shifted to planning for the capture of *Raja* and *Rani* posts.

The *Poonch-Haji Pir* road was dominated by two enemy posts called *Raja* and *Rani*. *Raja* Post was 1.5 km to the north of Indian *Post 405*. *Rani* Post was 1 km further to the north-west of *Raja*. These posts served as a staging camp for infiltrators into the *Poonch* sector. For India to establish the *Poonch-Uri* link fully, it was critical to secure these two posts.

2 SIKH, commanded by Lt. Col. NN Khanna was operating on *Chhamb-Jourian* sector and was singled out for *Operation Faulad* by the GOC of 15 Corps. On August 29, 1965, the battalion moved to *Poonch* after their gallant action in the *Battle of Chhamb*—for their series of swift and daring exploits with clinical precision tactics which led to the appropriation of ten enemy posts within three days! It was an astonishing feat and had considerably lifted the spirits of the soldiers. Apart from sending out patrols to protect the road, 2 SIKH used their War cry from the convoy vehicles to psyche out the enemy. They arrived in *Poonch* on August 30, 1965 and eagerly started preparations.

3 DOGRA was assigned to capture *Raja* by midnight of September 2, 1965 and 2 SIKH was tasked to capture *Rani* by 1000 hrs on September 3, 1965. However, the attack on *Raja* post on the night of September 1,

1965 could not achieve success due to stiff enemy opposition. The post was on a steep gradient, the last 200 metres was virtually a vertical wall. As if that wasn't an obstacle enough, the post was heavily mined and staunchly held.

Both the battalions had to march back for four hours to *Poonch* by first light on September 3, 1965. Non-capture of *Raja* post was becoming an obstacle to the well-laid plans. It was then that Lt. Col. Khanna volunteered to capture *Raja* Post (*Chand* as per Pakistan Army). Unfortunately, the time for recce had been reduced to just one night as the D-Day was brought forward by a day to September 5, 1965. This gave the unit less time to prepare and plan. Nevertheless, the unit gathered as much information about terrain and enemy disposition as was possible and then set out to achieve its objective. Both units marched five and a half hours to assembly areas. They planned to launch the attack on the piquet at 0400 hrs on September 6, 1965. Due to the difficult terrain it was pushed to 0500 hrs.

At 0500 hrs, the Battalion moved from the FUP amidst concentrated enemy artillery fire. The attack was launched from two directions—along the southern ridge and from the south-eastern slopes. They had to manoeuvre wire obstacles, watch out for mines and dodge the hail of consistent enemy fire. The valiant troops of 2 SIKH continued the assault unfazed and determined to take the combat to its logical conclusion. The difficult terrain and unending stream of enemy fire were causing a lot of casualties. By 0535 hrs all companies of 2 SIKH were pinned down below *Raja* post along the wire obstacles and minefields and there seemed to be no way to proceed ahead.

The attack had reached a state of limbo and combat inertia was setting in. Lt. Col. Khanna realised it was either do/die or a turnabout again. He stood up and waved his green and white jersey (a hallmark of high-altitude War school instructors) so that his troops could see him clearly. He shouted the unit War cry boldly "*Jo bole so Nihal, Sat Sri Akal*" and started climbing by himself towards *Raja* post with a grenade in his hand! This got the 2 SIKH troops flustered and they started climbing to follow their CO. This set a chain reaction of "*josh*" throughout the troops. With a great surge of spirit, and renewed vigour they forced the wire obstacle and cautiously ran across the minefields. The troops attacked the first bunker and then there was no stopping them. Lt. Col. Khanna too dashed across a mined area and threw a grenade into one of the enemy's forward bunkers destroying it. As he did so, he was hit by a burst of enemy fire in the chest.

Despite being mortally wounded, Lt. Col. Khanna continued to spur on his troops, and they gave full thrust to the assault, living up to the legendary zeal and bravado of 2 SIKH. Lt. Col. Khanna unfortunately died while being evacuated to the Regimental aid post. This gave the troops an even more determined approach to avenge their CO. They fought bravely—and How! Like men possessed! Their simmering rage on the death of their CO was taken out on the enemy—it was a wrathful, torturous battle as the enemy was equally determined not to be ousted. After three hours of dogged enforcement including hand-to-hand combat, 2 SIKH claimed their victory on *Raja*.

In another brave deed, Sepoy Jarnail Singh made a dash for the Pakistani platoon commander and they were both engaged in a duel. Both shot each other simultaneously and were killed in action. *Raja* was finally captured at 0710 hours, on September 7, 1965. The success signal was given at 0900 hrs.

Meanwhile 3 DOGRAS had rounded up *Rani* Post in a surprise attack on the enemy and the *Uri-Poonch* link-up was thereby completed on September 9, 1965. The link-up with Northern pincers was completed with the capture of *Kahuta* on September 10, 1965. This sealed the entire *Haji Pir* Sector. This turning point ensured that all enemy resistance in the bulge ceased and the military objectives in *Uri-Poonch* sector were achieved.

Notes

- Lt. Col. N. N. Khanna was awarded MVC (Posthumous) for gallantry. As one of the soldiers said "We won a Raja, and we lost a Raja"—*Raja Litta Raja Ditta.*
- 2 SIKH during the War continued valiant operations in *Poonch* sector and for its gallant action the Battalion was awarded the Battle Honour "Raja."

- Unfortunately, despite the hardship and loss of lives to capture this post, it too was returned to Pakistan post the Tashkent agreement between India and Pakistan.
- Punjab Chief Minister, Capt. Amarinder Singh has dedicated a room in his house to the valour of the 2nd Battalion of the Sikh Regiment (2 SIKH), in which he had served in his earlier days.

He will win whose Army is animated by the same spirit throughout all its ranks.

—Sun Tzu

September of Year 1965
Chhamb Sector

TURNING POINT 10

The Azure Sortie

Come September and the India-Pakistan War moved from the Earth to the Skies. The Indian Air Force got the opportunity to spread their wings which had been denied to them in the 1962 and previous wars.

The Indian Army had reached a precarious position in the *Chhamb* area as Pakistan Army had mounted a large offensive in the *Chhamb-Jourian* sector in the wee hours of the morning of September 1, 1965. Though the Indian troops had fought back valiantly and defended their positions, with supplies running out they were forced to withdraw to more secure bases to counter the three armours of Pakistan Army. Since reinforcements would have taken time to reach in the rough terrain, Air Force support was asked for. It only got approved by the evening of September 1.

The nearest IAF base at Pathankot had "Mystère IV" and "Vampire" aircraft and all assets were primed for the strike. The Vampire unfortunately was a WWII vintage, first generation jet fighter which had reached the end of its operational life. Owing to the precarious situation, the Vampire squadron commander decided to launch his near-obsolete aircraft despite being aware of the presence of PAF fighter CAP, as reported by intelligence over *Chhamb*. (It is said that IAF later admitted that using these ancient aircraft was a mistake at that time when better choice was available.)

The first wave of Vampires took off at dusk and struck Pakistan's armoury on reaching *Chhamb*. They were led by Squadron Leader SK

Dhar. They managed to have their moment of glory and created panic in the ranks of the Pakistan Army. (Unfortunately, they struck some of the Indian posts as well!)

The 12 DIV Commander of Pakistan Army urgently radioed for air support and a flight of two "Sabres" was dispatched from its CAP area to *Chhamb.* Pakistan Air Force planes were gunning for an aggressive confrontation and crossed the International Boundary to enter Indian airspace. IAF was not expecting PAF to violate the International boundary brazenly. The PAF Sabres intercepted the second formation of Vampires. Though outclassed, both in terms of technology and performance, the Vampires did their best and rose to the occasion by engaging the Sabres in a spectacular display of bravado and some intrepid moves. The Sabres used their superior agility and firepower to get the better of the Vampires and unsurprisingly shot down three of the archaic Vampires. Flt. Lt. Sondhi managed to escape.

Even though *Chhamb* was lost to the enemy that fateful day, the Indian Air Force strikes coupled with the tenacious defence by the Army's AMX-13 tanks succeeded in blunting the Pakistan Army's advance and the enemy could not proceed further.

The next day GNAT's were deployed and engaged the Pakistan Army in a grinding affray by carrying out strafing. This action halted the enemy advance for that time.

Though the IAF has been criticised for the use of Vampires to accomplish the task, it must be noted that the objective of distracting the enemy to halt their rapid advance into Indian territory was achieved due to the Vampires attack that day. This was a turning point in the War, and it was enabled by the IAF pilots strafing the enemy to prevent any further penetration into Indian territory. As events unfolded later, the enemy advance being contained on September 1, 1965 turned the tables and history was changed forever. If Pakistan Forces had continued their foray without being deflected by IAF the War would have been finished, then and there.

The IAF did withdraw the Vampires from the rest of the War though—in essence, they operated with reduction of combat strength by a good 35%. At the start of the War IAF was numerically superior compared to PAF but technologically below par.

Note

- "Rafiqui"—Sq. Ldr. Sarfaraz Rafiqui from PAF—was credited with shooting 2 of the Vampires. He was considered one of the plucky commanders at PAF and was admired by the Indians too for his prowess. He also led the Sabre attacks later on over *Halwara* (SW of Ludhiana) airbase on September 6, 1965 and was shot down when intercepted by Flying Officer AR Gandhi and Flying Officer PS Pingale who were on OROP. He was given Pakistan's highest Leadership award—Hilal-e-Jurat.

War alone brings up to their highest tension all human energies and imposes the stamp of nobility upon the peoples who have the courage to make it.

—Benito Mussolini

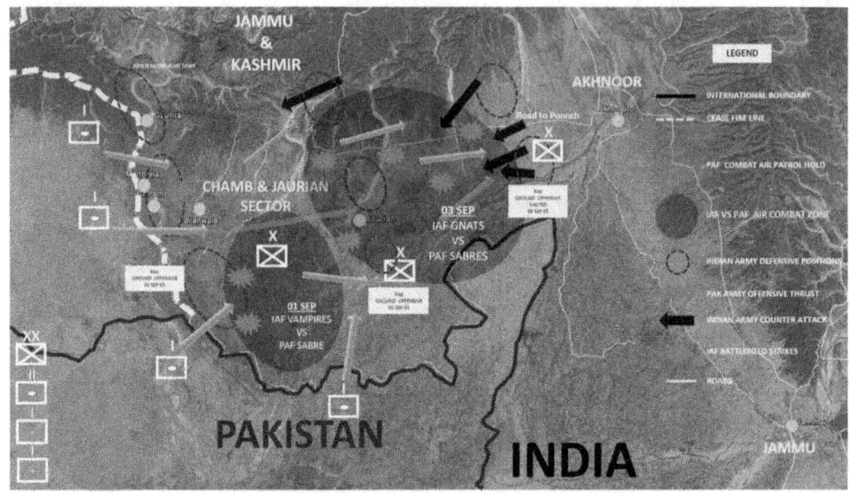

Source: https://theprint.in/defence/1965-india-pakistan-war-how-iafs-heroes-slayed-pafs-superior-sabre-fighter-jets/287642/

September of Year 1965
Mirpur-Chhamb POK

TURNING POINT 11

The Champions of the Cerulean Skies

In 1965, the Indian Air Force was still struggling with an obsolete fleet of Vampires, Toofanis and Mystère fighters. It had added a modest second-generation aircraft fleet of the Gnats, Hawker Hunters and the Canberra bombers, but the Hunters and the Gnats faced problems of gun stoppages.

On September 1, 1965 when Pakistan Army invaded India in *Chhamb* sector, the Indian Army had asked for air cover to engage the enemy. The Indian Air Force reacted within 30 minutes of the go-ahead received from HQ and entered the fray with four Vampires. The Vampires were unfortunately shot down by Pakistan Air Force. Thereafter, Indian Air Force decided to deploy Gnats to counter the sleek Sabres of the Pakistan Air Force. 23 SQUADRON (PANTHERS) of the Indian Air Force was given the privilege for the attack.

The Gnat was a lightweight fighter jet, and this gave it speed advantage as well as the fact that it was difficult to spot during combat. It did require a highly skilled pilot to fly it. The Gnat was well comparable to the Sabre of Pakistan Air Force, but the enemy had discounted the Gnat as a threat and considered the Hawker Hunter in IAF service as its main adversary. They were in for a rude shock—and a revised opinion.

The core of the specialist 23 SQN detachment of the IAF was made up of pilots with good air combat training and was commanded by Sq. Ldr. Johnny Greene "Greene"—a seasoned fighter pilot. The 23 SQN Gnats landed in *Pathankot* at dusk on September 2, 1965, undetected by the superior Pakistan radars. The team was apprised on the grim situation in *Chhamb* and the recent Vampire losses. The brief from the base commander was short and straight: "We want you to shoot down the Sabres. How you do it is your problem, but the Sabres will have to be tackled."

"Greene" hatched a risky and daring plan to trap the Pakistan Air Force Sabres—brassy and audacious. Four IAF Mystères (led by Sq. Ldr. Goodman) were to fly as "bait" at 5,000 ft to draw out the Sabres near *Chhamb.* They were to be followed by two, four-aircraft formations of Gnats flying low at 300 ft above ground level, far below the scanning eyes of Pakistan's *Sakesar* radar. "Wheels Up" was scheduled at 0600 hrs on September 3, 1965.

The first formation was led by "Greene" and had Flt. Lt. "Manna" Murdeshwar as his wingman. The other section leader consisted of Sq. Ldr. B. S. Sikand with Flt. Lt. "Pat" Pathania as his wingman. Trailing this formation by about 2,000 yards at 100 ft was the second of the four-aircraft Gnat formation led by Squadron Leader Trevor "Keelor," with Flt. Lt. "Kichha" Krishnaswamy as his wingman. Keelor's subsection consisted of Sq. Ldr. A. S. Sandhu, with Flying Officer P. S. Gill as his No. 2.

Wg. Cdr. Krishan Dandapani, based at IAF's *Amritsar* radar, was keenly following the route. His observation was to scan for any approaching enemy threat to the "bait" aircraft and he was glued to his radar screen. Soon he observed a blip and could make out a Starfighter heading for *Chhamb.* The entire plan hinged on the Pakistan Air Force taking the bait. A while later a four-aircraft Sabre formation blipped on Wg. Cdr. Dandapani's screen showing up at 30,000 feet, and accelerating towards *Chhamb.* He quickly transmitted the enemy aircraft positions to the IAF aircraft.

As per plan, the IAF formation of the Mystères turned left from *Akhnoor* Bridge and towards *Chhamb.* The arrival of the Mystères at *Chhamb* was picked up by Pakistan radar as anticipated, and predictably PAF dispatched the Sabres to greet the IAF boys. So, the Pakistan Air Force had taken the bait! The Game was on!

Wg. Cdr. Dandapani, on seeing the enemy aircraft closing in on the Mystères, gave the cue for the Mystères to pull out of the arena. The Mystères dutifully turned and exited from the battle zone in a clean getaway. And the Gnats then gleefully announced themselves to the enemy!

'Greene' initiated the greetings by climbing with his formation. This was the place where the Gnats were vulnerable to the Sabres but they kept a good look-out for them. The IAF pilots aimed to reach an aggressive height of 30,000 ft in less than ninety seconds. As 'Greene's' Gnats zoomed up, 'Keelor' and the pilots of the second formation eased up behind them and ensured they covered Greene's flank. Whilst 'Keelor' was climbing he perceived a Sabre, which was flown by Flt. Lt. Yousaf Khan of Pakistan Air Force. The Sabre was attempting to descend behind 'Manna' in 'Greene's' formation. 'Pat' also made contact with the threatening Sabre behind 'Manna'. Sq. Ldr. Greene's formation members swerved a hard right to break into the attacker's reported position.

Flt. Lt. Yousaf (PAF) struggled to persist behind 'Manna' in order to attempt a shot. 'Keelor' recognised this danger and took a turn to remain behind Flt. Lt. Yousaf (PAF). And then he took aim. The burst of fire from the Gnat hit home—the Sabre's right wing and elevator took the brunt. Then 'Keelor' quickly closed in on the Sabre and, firing closely at 200 yards, finished it off.

And that was the first Gnat kill in the world!

In the meantime, 'Pat', in 'Greene's' formation spotted the other section of Sabres dropping on the Gnats from 3,000 ft above. He decided to tackle them and kicked full throttle ahead of the Sabre. But halfway through his daring manoeuvre, he spotted tracers flying past his Gnat—and soon enough an F-104 Starfighter was visible, heading for him at a high speed! Taken aback, 'Pat' attempted to move away from the direct onslaught of bullets.

Whilst 'Keelor' was dispatching Flt. Lt. Yousaf's (PAF) Sabre, *Sakesar* radar control in Pakistan urgently drew the attention of two Starfighters towards *Chhamb*. The Sabres then made a quick getaway from the combat zone, accelerating towards Pakistan. The Gnats team decided to head back keeping in mind the low fuel indications.

This was a remarkable performance by the Indian Air Force boys. In less than a couple of minutes, the IAF Gnats had bandied with the best of what the PAF had thrown at them and emerged victorious. They had shot down one Sabre and were perilously close to trapping another two, but the untimely intervention of the Starfighter (PAF) saved the Sabres from the catastrophe. The Starfighter itself was at a vulnerable position and avoided getting shot down because it beat a hasty retreat from the battlefield. This was a remarkable turning point for India.

A delighted Arjan Singh, Marshal of the Indian Air Force is rumoured to have famously told the Defence Minister post the encounter, "Sir, please tell the Indian nation, on this day a Sabre Slayer is born!" That is how the appellation "Sabre Slayer" was given for the Gnat, which had taken part in the first air combat and emerged victorious.

There was, however, one casualty that day that dampened the spirits of the 23 SQN—Flt. Lt. Sikand's Gnat had a complete electrical failure and he got separated from the fight. He was unfortunately forced to make an emergency landing at the Pakistan Air Force field at *Pasrur*—which he thought was an abandoned Indian airfield. He spent the rest of the War as a POW.

23 SQUADRON went on to achieve more victories against the Pakistan Air Force in the coming days of the 1965 War. The Gnats held sway on the battlefield over *Chhamb* and other battle zones until the end of the War. The calibre and experience of IAF GNAT pilots was recognised and acknowledged by fighter pilot hang-outs all across the world.

Notes

- Flt. Lt. Pathania, who missed shooting down a Sabre on September 3, 1965, got a shot at a Sabre kill the next day near the *Akhnoor* bridge.
- Flt. Lt. "Kala" Sandhu, the talented "*Flying Sikh*" got a Sabre kill on September 18, 1965.
- The GNAT's issue of gun stoppage was a major deterrent to the IAF pilots as many of the pilots missed shooting down more PAF aircraft due to this problem in the coming days.
- Sq. Ldr. Greene, Sq. Ldr. Keelor, Flt. Lt. Pathania and Flt. Lt. Sandhu were awarded the coveted Vir Chakra each for their dare-devilry over the battlefields of the 1965 War.

In war there is no substitute for victory.

—Douglas MacArthur

September of Year 1965
Pakistan

TURNING POINT 12

The Wind beneath the Wings: Reconnaissance and Observer Missions

Many brave and intelligent Air Force officers contributed to the turning points in the War by the reconnaissance and photos that provided good information to their comrades on the ground and enabled the Army think tanks to plan their moves. Without the strategic information it would have been simply impossible for the Indian troops to proceed or make any headway. Most of these missions were done covertly using stealth approach and entailed flying undetected and at the same time evading flying shrapnel and gunfire—involving great personal risk and often compromising their own safety.

The most outstanding of these heroes were Wg. Cdr. Goodman and Wg. Cdr. Prem Singh who through some adventuresome ways and resourceful means managed to obtain good information in addition to leading their formations ably in active strafing and aerial combat.

Wg. Cdr. Goodman, commanding 31 Squadron flying the Mystère fighter-bomber aircraft from *Pathankot*, was entrusted with the task of destroying enemy tanks and troop concentrations in the *Chhamb* sector on the evening of September 1, 1965. The Squadron immediately went into action and blunted the enemy offensive by destroying tanks and armoured vehicles. Between September 2 and September 8, 1965 the Squadron undertook many reconnaissance and ground attack missions in the area. These included rocket attacks on tank concentrations at *Troti* and *Chhamb* and strafing of enemy positions at *Jourian*.

On September 9, 1965, the Squadron undertook the most commendable task. A photo recce and strike mission were undertaken between *Kasur* and *Raiwind* by two aircraft. They attacked a train carrying tanks and destroyed twenty of them. This was followed by an attack on a tank and heavy gun concentration at *Chawinda*. Many of these missions were led by Wg. Cdr. Goodman himself, against heavy air and ground opposition. The Squadron conducted a number of successful strikes on enemy positions.

Wg. Cdr. Prem Pal Singh was initially a Dakota pilot but later converted to the Canberra aircraft. During the War, Wg. Cdr. Prem Pal Singh Commanded 5 SQUADRON, "The Tuskers." The unit, equipped with the Canberra bomber, was assigned the triple task of tactical bombing, close air support and armed patrolling.

The TUSKERS carried out tactical bombing of various targets in order to destroy the Pakistan Air Force on ground. Led by Wg. Cdr. Prem Pal Singh himself, Pakistani Army camps east of *Gujarat* and airfields at *Chaklala*, *Dab*, *Murid*, *Akwal*, *Risalwala*, *Wagowal*, *Sargodha* and *Peshawar* were successfully attacked.

The Squadron also carried out close air support missions to the Army in *Kasur*, *Khem Karan*, *Pasrur*, *Chawinda* and *Sialkot* sectors. During the period of War, the Squadron undertook 39 sorties of armed patrolling over *Agra*, *Palam*, *Ambala*, *Halwara* and *Adampur.* Most of the operational missions over enemy territory were carried out during the hours of darkness. The targets were identified by moonlight. These dangerous operational sorties were undertaken in the face of heavy enemy anti-aircraft fire, with exceptional courage and determination.

Wg. Cdr. Prem Pal Singh was commanding a bomber squadron between September 6, 1965 and September 9, 1965 wherein he undertook six offensive and tactical close support operations, including reconnaissance over the *Sargodha*, *Dab*, *Akwal* and *Marud* airfields, marking of *Peshawar* airfield and bombing of Pakistani troop and armour concentrations. In the face of heavy anti-aircraft fire, he led the bombing and reconnaissance missions with courage, determination and tenacity.

The contribution of these missions by these gallant officers and others is immeasurable. These missions were responsible for turning around the situation for India by providing the needed information on enemy movements which was not provided by ground intelligence.

Notes

- Wg. Cdr. Goodman was awarded the Maha Vir Chakra for his gallantry, leadership, and professional skill.
- Wg. Cdr. Prem Pal Singh was awarded the Maha Vir Chakra for displaying a high sense of duty and gallantry. He subsequently rose to the rank of Air Marshal. He was awarded AVSM and PVSM for distinguished service

It is only the enlightened ruler and the wise general who will use the highest intelligence of the army for the purposes of spying, and thereby they achieve great results.

—Sun Tzu

September of Year 1965
Tithwal Sector

TURNING POINT 13

The Storming Heroes of Tithwal

In September 1965, the Pakistanis were still in control of a large tract east of the *Kishanganga*, which was being continuously used for infiltration into the Kashmir Valley. *Kishanganga* is located in the Bandipore district of J&K. Three bridges over the river gave free access from the west bank, and the Pakistanis made good use of them.

The Kishanganga River becomes the Neelam River when it enters Pakistan. To deny the infiltrators further access to the territory east of the *Kishanganga*, 104 Infantry Brigade of the Indian Army was ordered to drive out the Pakistanis from the area and destroy the bridges. One of the first objectives of 104 Infantry Brigade was *Sanjoi*. *Sanjoi* lies 3 miles north of *Tangdhar*. At a height of 9,000 ft this enemy piquet provided an easy observation of the lower Indian piquets and was an obstruction for the Indian Army movements. The task to capture this feature was the prerogative of 3/8 GORKHA RIFLES.

The *Sanjoi* feature was a laborious and strenuous climb. It was literally an uphill task for the Gorkhas as the terrain had no paths ear-marked and the troops had to grope their way around labyrinthine terrain. Many a time they resorted to crawling their way ahead. They did a thorough reconnoitre and then launched an attack on the night of September 3, 1965.

In a swashbuckling move the Gorkhas surrounded the piquet, and, as expected, they received retaliatory fire but with far worse force than they had anticipated. The Company commander Maj. Verma and his entire section were unfortunately shot. Some soldiers ran into the mines in haste and were instantly killed. In all this melee, Lance Naik Raj Bahadur Gurung used his initiative and climbed a pine tree he spied and using it as a saddle boldly launched himself on the roof of an enemy bunker. He tossed a grenade in that bunker from the rear. He then proceeded to swiftly kill the enemy gunners manning the bunker with only his "Khukri" before they could shout out an alert. Lance Naik Gurung then set about making an opening in the wall—all the time ensuring he was dodging bullets and not coming under enemy eyes. The Gorkhas poured in through the wall opening, raring for blood and determined to avenge their fallen comrades. It was a ruthless hand-to-hand assault and the Gorkhas made good of the enemy, living up to their valiance and prowess. The enemy could not bear this killer attack and abandoned their post to save their lives.

By September 4, 1965, 3/8 GORKHA RIFLES was the proud possessor of three enemy posts at *Sanjoi*. The enemy launched two furious counterattacks on the nights of September 4 and September 6, which were both repulsed.

The next objective of the brigade was a feature overlooking the *Kishanganga*: *Point 9013*. The task of capturing it was given to 4 KUMAON, and the battalion concentrated at *Bhatija* (10,100 ft) on September 14, 1965 in preparation for the attack.

Point 9013 is a hill feature in *Tithwal* sector. It dominated the *Sanjoi* feature and, occupied by an enemy post, wreaked havoc on the Indian troops. Its capture was essential for continued Indian operations in the area. Lieutenant Colonel Salick decided to attack the feature from the *Sairagali* side with his B and C Companies, keeping D Company in reserve. It was to be a silent attack, though the battalion had adequate artillery support on call. *Point 9013* was well-defended with wire obstacles, mined approach and fortified bunkers. The enemy was keen to retain this post at all costs.

The assault was planned for 0200 hrs on September 20, 1965. It was a simple plan wherein a patrol of ten men under 2/Lt. Verma was to create a diversion by moving from lower *Sanjoi* feature to the base of *Point 9013*. They were to also shout the War cry and give the impression that there was an attack from south-west of *Point 9013*. The actual attack was to launch from the north-east direction. 'C' company was to lead the advance and 'B' Company was to follow. 'D' company was to support the attack with gunfire. Unfortunately, the start was not very auspicious. 'C' company took along the Intelligence Officer (a complete no-no) to guide them on the route. The troops were jittery with the numerous counterattack gunfire of the enemy and despite being briefed about the plan they mistook the movements of their comrades as that of the enemy and started firing back! This unfortunately gave away the position of the troops to the enemy and they started firing. The 'C' Coy troops also took a wrong turn and ended up in the river (nallah) bed. The Company Commander also did not display any enthusiasm, nor did he motivate or calm his troops. Since dawn was breaking, Lt. Col. Salick decided to delay the mission and ordered both companies to return to *Sanjoi*. The enemy in the meantime expecting an attack from Indian troops were busy firing shots all through the night and trying to figure out where the assault would be coming from!

Back at *Sanjoi*, 4 KUMAON troops were a dejected lot, they did not partake of any meals nor indulged in bonhomie with their comrades. The soldiers had prepared for a battle and not being able to achieve the target assigned was depressing. The next day the CO decided on a frontal attack approach—a silent attack. He was banking on the element of surprise to work in their favour. This time he ordered 'B' company to lead. Lt. Col. Salick personally shook hands with each soldier and boosted their sagging spirits and pumped up their morale. It was a dark night and the troops went in single file formation, slowly inching their way forward. They had to move cautiously, since the enemy was already on the alert and expecting them to attack and they could not afford to give away their positions, else they would be massacred. It was a dark, dreary night and the forward movement was slow as they had to watch out for sporadic mines too and ensure they remained on track. The enemy was uneasy and uptight already as the attack they had expected the night before had not happened and neither had they been able to sleep all night expecting a charge any time.

The leading platoon of B Company under Jemadar Ram Singh hit an enemy minefield shortly after midnight (September 21). Despite being wounded, the brave JCO painstakingly dragged his wounded foot and edged forward to find a way through the mines. He had successfully reached the barbed wires which signaled the end of the minefield and just as the watching platoon was about to breathe a sigh of relief, his dragging foot stepped on another mine!

The troops behind watched in horror, unable to do anything as the courageous JCO was flung across with the impact. His men wanted to dash to his help and some of them managed to follow the path he had taken. Treading cautiously they reached him, but he died soon after from his injuries and excessive bleeding. The rest of the men then used the path and moved across the minefield quickly. Unfortunately, there was no time to mourn. The platoon was well aware that it was the sheer grit of their intrepid platoon commander that the rest of the team could cross the minefield safely and save precious time. Now, they were even more determined to get the enemy.

The 'B' Coy platoon reached the base at dawn and were at FUP at 0730 hrs. But 'C' company was not there! It seemed the 'C' Company Commander (Capt. Gurbaksh Singh) was gripped with fear and deliberately chose not to participate in this battle! This was a huge setback but 'B' Coy Cdr, Capt. Shah did not want to abort the mission and decided to take a huge risk and proceed through with the mission operating with only his number of men! There was already so much delay and Capt. Shah did not want to wait up any more especially since the enemy had a whiff about their plans and could possibly be getting reinforcements.

At 0745 hrs he signaled for the assault to commence. The enemy was not expecting a daylight attack, and were busy going about their morning chores. They had kept a vigil all night and were sleep deprived and weary. Capt. Shah and his men burst upon the enemy from the undergrowth and the silence was broken only by their resounding War cry. The delay in the attack actually worked in favour of 4 KUMAON who set about extracting vengeance for the previous night too! They were men thirsty for a combat and attacked the bunkers, opened fire, and caused the enemy to flee after a grueling battle that raged for almost three hours.

Captain Shah was wounded twice but refused to be evacuated till after the battle. The KUMAONI's tenacity ultimately won the day and the hill was in their hands at 1015 hrs. Sepoy Kewla Nand was wounded in the initial assault but kept up with his platoon. He spotted two enemy soldiers attempting to flee and made a beeline for them. Though he managed to knock out one, he was killed by the other.

2/Lt. Khare pursued the fleeing enemy not realising he was the lone hunter. The enemy hiding in the forest engaged him in volatile fire and bullets ripped his stomach. He struggled back somehow and his comrades, seeing his condition, were further provoked to hunt the rest of the enemy down and finish them off. The success signal was sent soon after. The troops anticipated a counterattack which came within the half hour and was successfully repulsed. Another counterattack put in after more preparation was also repelled though it incurred high casualties for the Kumaons.

There were no more shelling and counter-fires post the announcement of the Ceasefire on September 22, 1965. These captures turned the situation around by ensuring that the enemy was completely kept at bay until the ceasefire.

Notes

- To commemorate the Kumaonis' victory at Point 9013, the hill was named the Kumaon Hill.
- For conspicuous gallantry in the action, Captain Surendra Shah received the Vir Chakra. Another recipient of this award was Naik Chander Singh.
- Lt. Khare recovered from his wound and rejoined 4 KUMAON six months later. He also served in the 1971 War later.

War can only be abolished through war -in order to get rid of the gun it is necessary to take up the gun.

—Mao Zedong

… And to the Plains of Punjab

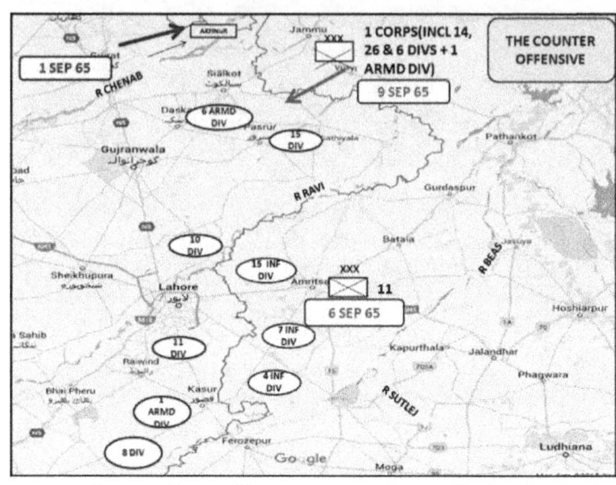

Source: https://images.news18.com/ibnlive/uploads/2015/09/1965warmap.jpg

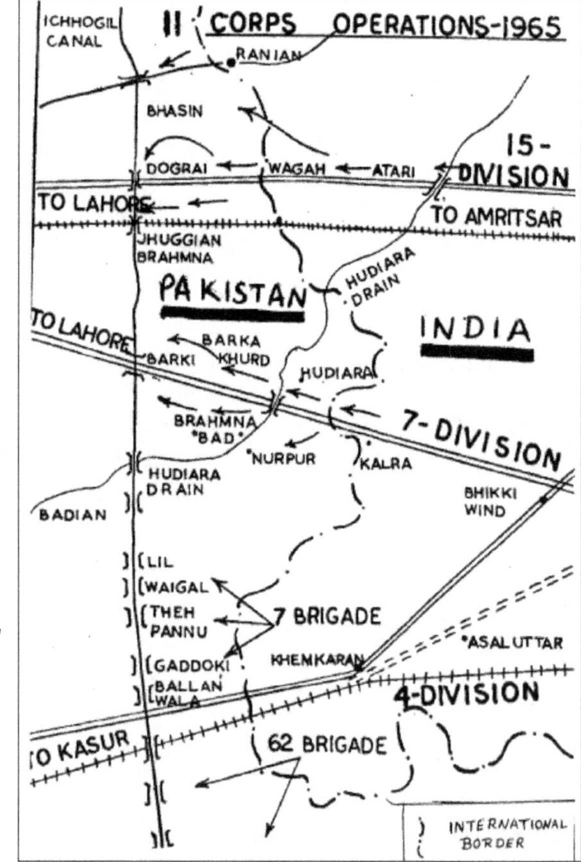

The axis of attacks were:
15th Infantry Division along the GT road on Amritsar-Lahore axis.
7th Infantry Division along Khalra-Barki-Bhikkiwind Axis
4th Mountain Division along Khemkaran-Kasur Axis.

Source: http://indiandefence.com/threads/great-battles-14-asal-uttar-1965-turn -of-the-tide.56928/

September of Year 1965
Lahore Sector

TURNING POINT 14

13 km to Lahore: Lahore Front

India's Defence Minister Y. B. Chavan made a startling announcement in his speech in the Lok Sabha on September 6, 1965. He confirmed to the Country and to the World that "India had crossed the international border" in the *Lahore* sector. And this was the start of an all-out War. There was not even a hint of apology in that announcement. India had taken enough, and with none of the World leaders intervening nor the United Nations responding to pleas to stop the forceful foray of Pakistan Forces into Her territories, India had to take the matter into Her own hands.

The last straw had broken this camel's back when on the afternoon of September 5, 1965, Pakistani aircraft intruded across the international boundary at *Wagah* near *Amritsar* and fired rockets at an Air Force unit. Strong retaliatory action from the IAF succeeded in driving them away. This violation was reported but despite that there were still further encroachments over the same border by the Pakistan Air Force. It seemed that Pakistan's next move was to attack Punjab (this was proved right in time to come) across the international border.

Offence being the best defence, it was also necessitated by the need to open a different battleground to divert the focus from *Chhamb* and as well to forestall the opening of another front by Pakistan. And this time was the best opportunity to launch "Operation Riddle" which had been in the plotting stage for a while by the politico-military leadership of India.

The offensive under the overall direction of Lt. Gen. Harbaksh Singh, GOC Western Command was taken in *Sialkot*, *Khem Karan* and *Lahore* sectors.

XI Corps operations had planned an advance towards *Lahore* along three axes—*Amritsar-Lahore, Khalra-Burki-Lahore* and *Khem Karan-Kasur* roads. The Indian plan envisaged a limited offensive intended to cover the area from *Dera Baba Nanak* in the north to the *Sutlej* in the south. It may be noted here that as early as 1950, Pakistan had constructed a multipurpose waterway—the BRB link canal also known as *Ichhogil canal*—as a strong defensive measure and it was in this terrain that the Indian Forces under XI Corps were planning to operate.

At 0400 hrs on September 6, 1965, 54 Infantry Brigade crossed the international boundary. The 3 JAT unit of the Brigade vigorously attacked the objective on *Mile 14* on the *Amritsar-Lahore* road and managed to capture it by 0630 hrs, less than two hours after the launch of "Operation Riddle"! Buoyed by early success, the JATS persisted ahead and in the next half hour had another victory—the village of *Gosal-Dial.* In this attack, 3 JAT seized weapons and POWs.

The forward positions were lightly held by Pakistan Forces, since they had not really anticipated a full-fledged Indian attack in this sector. The Pakistanis were taken by surprise, but considering the threat to their premier city, they convened quickly.

15 Division of 1 Corps managed to reach the *Ichhogil canal* and occupied its east bank. In an extraordinary feat, 3 JAT captured *Batapore* on the outskirts of *Lahore* by 1130 hrs that morning! Their joy was short-lived as no reinforcements came to shore up their strength despite a considerable wait, and they had no choice but to pull back to their launch point—a seriously huge loss of opportunity. The failure of the senior leadership to consolidate these successes was irreparable. Had they chosen to build on these wins *Lahore* could have possibly been taken then.

On September 6, 1965, Maj. Gen. Niranjan Prasad (GOC 15 INF DIV) had conveyed to Lt. Gen. Harbaksh Singh (who was finding the progress of the troops extremely slow and therefore enquired) that the situation at his end was risky and further advance of troops was impossible. The Corps Commander was not convinced and rushed to *Atari* himself. A quick assessment indicated otherwise. Lt. Gen. Harbaksh Singh relieved Maj. Gen. Prasad of his responsibility soon thereafter as he was alarmed at the lack of motivation and the lack of will to crusade. He felt that such a mindset was not contributory to uplifting the morale of the men. "A defeatist attitude seldom wins a War," he felt.

While the offensives by 15 and 7 Infantry Divisions progressed as planned, the 4 Infantry Division offensive along the *Khem Karan-Kasur* Axis encountered firm impediment as they ran into Pakistan's 1 Armoured Division. 1 Armoured DIV (Pakistan Army) had secretly concentrated in *Kasur* Sector and was getting ready to launch an offensive against India, along the same axis!

4 Infantry Division stalled its assailment plan and took up base in the village of *Asal Uttar*, a few kilometres from *Khem Karan* and then prepared its defensive strategy. Here both opposing forces had misread the opponent's move. While India was quick to modify its plan, Pakistan troops rushed headlong into the *Asal Uttar* trap and the rest is history.

Meanwhile, along the *Amritsar-Lahore* and *Khalra-Burki-Lahore* axis, 4 SIKH won a decisive battle at *Barki.*

In a move that remains contentious, the Army Commander had ordered 4 SIKH to be withdrawn from *Barki* and moved to 4 Mountain Division for the capture of *Khem Karan.* It was assessed (wrongly) that the position would fall easily into Indian hands. The plan entailed an attack on *Khem Karan* by 2 MAHAR—a unit which was freshly inducted and still moving into the area, with 4 SIKH behind *Khem Karan* to prevent the Pakistanis from escaping.

It may be noted here that 4 SIKH was the erstwhile 36th SIKHS under British India and is famous for the heroic battle of *Sarahgarhi* till last man standing on September 12 in 1897 when just 21 Sikh soldiers fought Afghan tribes of estimated 20,000-24,000 men (the film "Kesari" is based on this last stand). Military historians around the world consider it as history's greatest last stand. September 12 is commemorated every year by 4 SIKH as "Saragarhi Day."

Despite the adverse situation, the Army Commander was enthused with the hope to capture *Khem Karan* on September 12, as he wanted it to coincide with the *Saragarhi* Battle Honour Day of 4 SIKH. This was a gross miscalculation as the Pakistanis had a strong defence at *Khem Karan* complete with armour support. 4 SIKH soldiers, despite being battle weary from the fray at *Barki*, were made to move for a bold attempt for *Khem Karan* right after *Barki*, the night of September 10/11—and without realising unfortunately ran into a Pakistani tank harbour. Much to their chagrin they were all quickly captured along with their CO as they were in no position for combat having shed their RCL guns en route as the guns hindered their progress due to the heavy load. There was a railway line in front and a road at the back—they were badly trapped! Better judgement prevailed and to avoid a massacre the men surrendered. Some soldiers managed to escape and make their way to Indian posts unnoticed by the enemy, but they were hardly many. "The victors of *Barki*," were now taken prisoners, including their valorous commanding officer Lt. Col. Anant Singh! When the ceasefire took effect on September 23, *Khem Karan* remained in enemy hands.

On the other side, the Indian units continued their advance, and by September 22, had reached the *Ichhogil Canal* protecting the city of *Lahore*. Once the ceasefire was announced, two Pakistani companies attempted to re-occupy the eastern bund of the *Ichhogil Canal* on September 22, 1965. 9th battalion of the Madras regiment (as part of 65 INF BDE), under the command of Lt. Col. B. K. Satyan repulsed the attempt and in a daring, perilous move around midnight, attacked the enemy. The youngsters of the regiment, with excitement running high, assailed the enemy with swiftness and a reckless abandon that is so associated with the youth, and clobbered the enemy good.

One such warrior was "Uniyal," an energetic fighter who was the first to lead his platoon into the battle. He led his men eagerly, with a dash of brazenness right into the Bund. They were right away exposed to tracers from enemy guns. When they reached within two hundred yards of the objective, they encountered loaded fire and missiles from a pill-box somewhat to the north of the desired objective. This steady barrage of fire from the enemy held up the progress of the platoon. "Uniyal" realised that clearing this enemy position was essential for his troops to advance further. He had but a few seconds to decide his next move, and, without further thought, "Uniyal" was soon on his hands and knees with his men and crawling forward! Sepoy Narayanan and Sepoy Bhaskaran were two volunteers of the platoon, who under the cover of the tall grass, crawled ahead to silence the enemy guns—which they achieved within twenty minutes!

This gave the impetus for the rest of the platoon to dash forward. In a few and rapid strokes, the 9 MADRAS tackled their adversaries and occupied the pill-box—thereon they continued the blitz and surged ahead to clear every trench. Shouting their War cry of "Veer Madrasi" the MADRASIS were busy expending the enemy—even hurling them into the canal many a time! The MADRASI tigers were in their element and even came down to a hand-and-fist fight with the enemy. After a cut-throat and vicious clash, the battalion had their objective in 2.5 hours.

There were many more skirmishes that were not without some anxious moments. The lack of follow-up and the inadequacy to plan for contingencies was showing up at several points. Differences in senior leadership of the Indian Army resulted in loss of precious days and this gave the enemy time enough to regroup their strength and buttress up reinforcements.

The Indian troops were well within striking distance of *Lahore*, but the triumph was to be short-lived. It must be noted here that the aim given out by the Army HQ and Western Command was to threaten *Lahore* and not capture or occupy it. The explanation was simple. A threat to *Lahore* would force the Pakistani army to withdraw some of its rampaging forces from the *Chhamb-Jourian* sector and divert them towards protecting its premier city. Which is exactly what happened. This was a turning point for the Chhamb theatre as the enemy's attention was diverted to the Punjab sector. The opportunity to drive home the point that India will no longer accept transgressions on her territory was well made.

Notes

What happened to the 4 SIKH POW?

The 4 SIKH once they were captured were exposed to unmentionable torture, mental agony, gruesome interrogation, and starvation in the hands of the enemy. It is said that the grace of a nation can be truly seen in the way they treat (or don't) another human being, especially POW, and by this yardstick the enemy was totally devoid of any grace.

The unit was sent to *Lahore* with their hands tied and they were blind-folded. They went through a horrible ordeal wherein each soldier was locked up in a separate cell which had no lights, no windows, and poor air filled with odours. The soldiers were so acutely exhausted and battle fatigued, that they longed to sleep but were not allowed to do so by their captors. They were hounded and interrogated separately and at any time of day or night. They were also subject to brutal treatment, intimidated and hit as well as spoken to in foul language.

The 4 SIKH soldiers bore this persecution somehow and conducted themselves with dignity and did their best to maintain their sanity. The enemy broke all sense of decency by calling international media and proclaiming how well they were treating POWs! A photo of a Pakistani JCO hugging an Indian soldier was celebrated the world over on how well conducted the Pakistan Army was—if only they knew! Unfortunately, the inhuman crimes came to light only when the prisoners were repatriated.

The Indian POWs were subsequently sent to *Rawalpindi* jail and then to Kohat Fort. At each place, they were made to go through the utmost agony by their captors—intimidation, deafening noise, food not fit for human consumption, extreme mental trauma—and the list of inhuman treatment goes on—the brave soldiers endured this for months. Luckily, the International Red Cross intervened and got POW allowance organised which could at least fetch them some essential food items. In February 1966, after much lobbying these soldiers boarded a train to India to be repatriated and were finally reunited with their families and comrades.

It is said that Lt. Gen Harbaksh Singh personally apologised to Lt. Col. Singh on his return for pushing the fatigued men to go to *Khem Karan* on that fateful day.

Courage is contagious. When a brave man takes a stand, the spines of others are often stiffened.

—Billy Graham

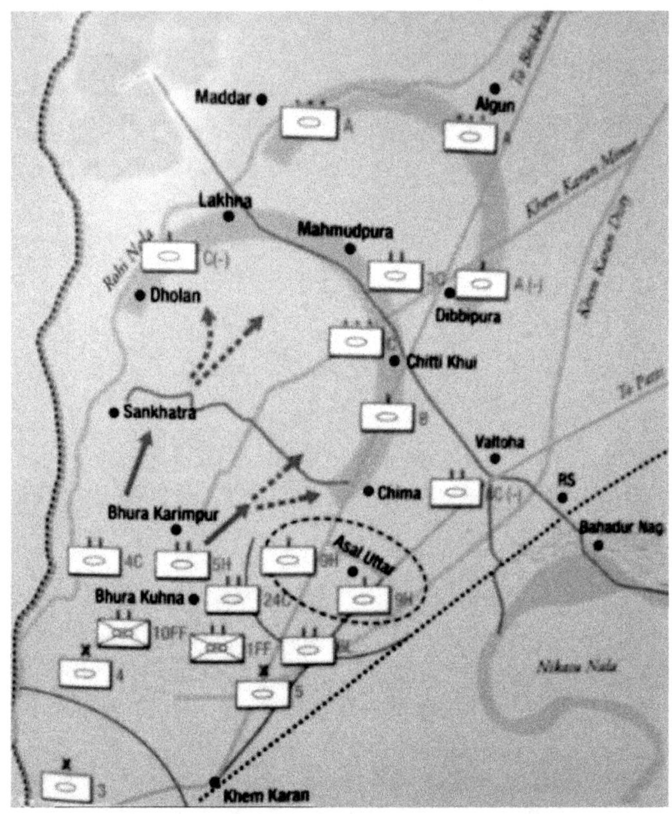

Source: http://indiandefence.com/threads/great-battles-14-asal-uttar-1965-turn-of-the-tide.56928/

September of Year 1965
Khem Karan Sector

TURNING POINT 15

The Befitting Reply: The Battle of Assal Uttar

In the backdrop of the *Chhamb* offensive by Pakistan Army (the failed "Operation Grand Slam"), the Indian Army launched its offensive action by crossing the International Border and threatening *Sialkot* and *Lahore* to relieve pressure on the *Chhamb-Jourian-Akhnoor* sector. While 1 Corps carried out offensive operations in *Sialkot*, XI corps launched a limited attack on September 6, 1965 on *Lahore-Amritsar* axis with its 15, 7, and 4 INF Divisions aimed at establishing a forward defence line-up to *Ichhogil* Canal—hitherto considered Pakistan's best defence asset.

Khem Karan is a town in *Majha* region of Punjab and part of *Amritsar* district. *Khem Karan* (India) and *Kasur* (Pakistan), each 5 km from the border, were connected by a road (not maintained since Partition) and the main obstacles between the two sides were the *Ichhogil Canal* and the *Rohi Nala*. Both towns were well-connected to extensive road networks of their countries.

4 MTN DIV of XI Corps was tasked to capture *Ichhogil* Canal from *Bedian* to *Lohgarh* and were given one Armoured regiment of 9 HORSE (Deccan Horse) equipped with Sherman tanks for the support of Infantry cover. Their task was to blow the bridge from *Kasur* to *Khem Karan* over the canal.

4 Mountain DIV (7 MTN BDE and 62 MTN BDE) began the attack on September 6, 1965 but surprisingly faced a stiff counterattack by Pakistan's 11 INF DIV. The Indian troops instead of battling a single

Infantry Brigade of the enemy (as they had anticipated), were being counterattacked by two Infantry Brigades of the Pakistan army as well as its "elite" 1st Armoured Division! This indicated that Pakistan Forces had been preparing to launch a full-fledged offensive on India from that sector! The Pakistanis had kept their huge contingent of American tanks hidden in a newly raised jungle in *Kasur* (Pakistan), near the Punjab border. Their plan of offence entailed capture of Indian territory up to the *Beas* River, and laying siege to *Amritsar* and beyond!

Seriously outnumbered now, the Indian troops ended up doing a disorderly withdrawal to *Assal Uttar* where they prepared to stand against the oncoming onslaught, and sensibly changed tactics from offensive approach to defensive. *Asal Uttar* was a village 7 km north of *Khem Karan* and 12 km from the border in *Tarn Taran* district of Punjab, India.

Asal Uttar was important for India as once Pakistan Army crossed it, their tanks would have a free reign on the flat terrains ahead. The natural rivers which were obstacles hitherto for the enemy would end up helping to secure their thrust. This would easily enable them to spread out quickly, making it difficult for any Indian defence to contain them since the expanse would allow the enemy to launch multiple armoured thrusts from different directions. The Indian troops at that time lacked sufficient armour and would not have been able to counter adequately for it would be some time before reinforcements could be moved. It was imperative for the Indian troops to somehow stop further advance of the enemy then and there and not allow the enemy tanks to break out into the Punjab plains.

When Pakistan Armed Forces crossed into India from the Punjab border at *Khem Karan* on September 6, 1965, their 1st Armoured Division and 11th Infantry Division captured the town of *Khem Karan*. Pakistan Army aimed to capture Beas bridge too. This was a clever strategy to isolate the Indian Forces from the subcontinent, lay siege to *Amritsar* and then take over the entire Country. (Their plan had ear-marked September 15, 1965 for capture of New Delhi!)

It may be noted here that the Indian side participated in the War with old Centurion tanks and Sherman 4 tanks. The Pakistan Army came with Patton tanks which were much superior.

At *Assal Uttar*, the Indian troops had camouflaged themselves in the sugarcane fields. The soldiers had a lot of solidarity from the villagers. The benevolent villagers many a time risked their lives to get food and water for the soldiers—often even crawling through the fields—that kindness was remembered for years to come by soldiers and officers alike.

D-day for the Pakistani push was scheduled to be September 7, 1965, which was, however, delayed by a day due to the damage caused to the bridge on *Rohi Nala*. This delay gave India's 4 Mountain Division enough time to lay the area around with mines.

Pakistan Army launched their offensive on the morning of September 8, 1965 at 0830 hrs. Their attack on the central axis was thwarted by the Infantry battalions of 1/9 GORKHA RIFLES, 4 GRENADIERS and 9 JAMMU AND KASHMIR RIFLES. Even though at one point in the battle the Indian Forces were outflanked, the tanks of the advancing Pakistani Army were engaged by India's DECCAN HORSE. It must be noted that the shenanigans engagement deployed atypical and unconventional means which did rattle the Indian troops but could not erode their spirits.

As enemy tanks broke through the Indian defences, Lt. Col Caleb (CO 3 CAV) and his troops intercepted them on the *Bhikhiwind-Khem Karan* road and in the ensuing skirmish destroyed 6 enemy tanks. The enemy was again curbed as it moved towards the west and soon enough its advance was halted for that day. This hampered any further advance of the enemy to propel further and they were forced to retreat from that area.

After the initial failed thrust Pakistan Army again attacked at 1400 hrs and tried to outflank the Indian defences. However, from the north side too this thrust was countered by the tanks of 3 CAV, which faced the brunt of Pakistan's armoured thrust but was ably supported by other Armoured regiments—8 CAV and DECCAN HORSE.

At 0200 hrs on September 9, 1965, Pakistan Army Patton tanks assaulted the Indian contingent of 18 RAJ RIF but they could not push further as they encountered minefields and therefore withdrew. At dawn, Pakistan Air Force was brought in with strong artillery fire but by then Indian troops had set up their bunkers.

In the morning there were heavy attacks on 4 GRENADIERS, and they retaliated well under Lt. Col. Bhatti. 18 RAJ RIF was again subjected to tank and infantry fire, but they fought back with the support of DECCAN HORSE. At 2200 hrs the Pakistani Forces withdrew. Casualties were many on both sides.

Brigadier Theograj (Commander of 2nd Independent Armoured Brigade which included 3 CAV, DECCAN HORSE and 8 CAV) too had arrived on the scene. A mass armour thrust from the enemy was inevitable and meeting it head on would be suicidal. Along with Lt. Col. Caleb he prepared an ambuscade. They were aware that the great North Indian plains would hardly rebuff a rolling armoured column and hence came up with the ingenious solution of breaching the *Rohi Nala* and flooding the areas to the south and south-west of the sector making it a swampy terrain. There were no further attacks by the enemy that night—the proverbial calm before the storm!

Brig. Theograj and Lt. Col. Saleem Caleb positioned the Centurion squadrons in two concentric horseshoe shaped semicircles contrived to bring the firepower of the entire regiment to direct on the incoming enemy armour in a lethal crossfire, whilst also providing defence in depth. 'B' and 'C' squadrons formed the first semicircle from *Dholan* to *Chima* with *Mahmudpura* in the centre. Then 'A' Squadron formed the second semicircle. They were all well-camouflaged. The sugarcane fields had been well-entrenched with water by the Indian troops all through the night.

As anticipated, the Pakistani attack began in the morning of September 10, 1965 at 0800 hrs, initiated by one battalion of Pakistani Army supported by Patton tanks which attacked the 4th GRENADIER positions ahead of village *Chima*. They launched an intense artillery bombardment and by 0900 hrs the enemy tanks had managed to permeate the forward company positions and the situation was getting troublesome for Indian Forces.

Quartermaster Hamid (4th GRENADIER) observing this, realised the dire situation and fathomed that if the enemy tanks were not taken care of, it would all be over soon. Previously, on September 9, Hamid had destroyed two Patton tanks with the help of his jeep mounted RCL gun and had essentially become an eyesore for Pakistani soldiers. From the corner of his eye, QM Hamid spied a group of enemy Pattons heading towards the battalion defences. Without caring for his life, he immediately moved out to the flank with his gun mounted on a jeep.

In a daring reckless gambit, QM Hamid knocked out an approaching tank and quickly changing his position sent another tank up in flames! Speed was the name of his game and he was all over the battlefield. The substantial explosions around him did not deter him, nor the volley of shells whizzing past his ears, and he continued his firing—incredibly knocking out three Patton tanks back-to-back. He now became the attention of the enemy tanks and they collectively zeroed in on him once they spotted him. He was subjected to concentrated machine fire and was mortally wounded by a high explosive shell, but he still managed to slap the enemy in the face by dislodging a fourth tank before breathing his last!

This raw courage under fire was awe-inspiring and it fired up his comrades—courage is indeed contagious! The GRENADIERS put up a tough defiance and made the enemy run. There was no further attempt by the enemy in that sector. At the other end, Maj. Sandhu had perched himself in the rooftop of one of the houses in the village and was relaying enemy movement to his comrades—no one was taking any chances as it was now or never!

The Indian troops now made out as though they were withdrawing. The Pakistan Army took the bait and in the thrill of the chase to capture the Indians, drove their Patton tanks straight into the huge horseshoe-shaped formation set up in *Mahmudpura* (a field near the village of *Assal Uttar*). Since the Indian Forces had opened the dykes and small dams built on the streams and canals flowing through the region in the night as planned, the entire region had become waterlogged. Now the mighty tanks of Pakistan Army got stuck in slush and mud. Patton tanks are designed to engage in long-range duels and at close range they are basically just transport. They became sitting ducks for the smaller Indian force. Ninety-nine Patton tanks and several Sherman tanks were destroyed by the Indian Forces. The Commander of the Pakistani intrusion Maj. Gen. Naseer Ahmed Khan too was killed in action.

This battle was a turning point in the Indo-Pakistan War—it tilted the victory clearly towards India through better tactics, successful strategy, and the sheer force of assault. Strangely "Asal Uttar" means "befitting reply" or "Sahi Jawab" and that is what the Pakistan Forces with their sleek machines and tanks got—it was simply man versus machine. It was a people's War too—many deeds of valour were not only by men in uniform. Young farmers had risked their lives and by crawling up to the Indian soldiers despite dangerous bombardment by the enemy, bringing their humble offerings—rotis, buttermilk and even sweets!—they were aware that the troops had gone without food for days.

It may be appreciated that had QM Hamid not distracted the enemy tanks on that fateful day, they would have done a clean sweep of the Indian troops in that sector and would have had a clear run to *Amritsar*. It is also speculated that COAS Gen. Chaudhuri had wanted to replace 4 MTN DIV on September 10 and had wanted the Indian troops to fall back further to the Beas river, but this plan was opposed by his GOC Western Command Lt. Gen. Harbaksh Singh, who luckily had the foresight and the gall to see the ineffectiveness of that movement.

Notes

- Lieutenant Pervez Musharraf participated in this battle as part of Pakistan Army Artillery in the 16 Field Regimen, 1st Armoured Div—Artillery. He later became Chief of Army Staff and subsequently President of Pakistan. Gen. AS Vaidya, who commanded an IA tank regiment as a Lieutenant Colonel went on to head the command of the Indian Army.
- This battle has been recorded as the largest tank battle in history and the site of battle led to the creation of Patton Nagar. It well compares with the Battle of Kursk between Nazi Germany and the Soviet Union in the Second Word War.
- Lt. Col. Caleb received the Mahavir Chakra for leading his forces with rare foresight and courage.
- A 3-Rupee stamp commemorating Hamid was issued by India Post on January 28, 2000.

- Abdul Hamid was honoured with PVC posthumously—India's highest Military award, for his unmatched bravery during the battle of *Asal Uttar*. On the outskirts of *Chima* (a village neighbouring *Assal Uttar*), lies the final resting place of Company Quartermaster Havildar Abdul Hamid. One of the villagers Paiara Singh and his family is the caretaker of Hamid's grave and also a memorial the Army set up to honour the heroic soldier.
- 3rd Cavalry added to its name the sobriquet *Patton Wreckers.*
- The battle of Asal Uttar is taught as a battle strategy in all major War colleges in the world.

The general who advances without coveting fame and retreats without fearing disgrace, whose only thought is to protect his country and do good service for his sovereign, is the jewel of the kingdom.

—Sun Tzu

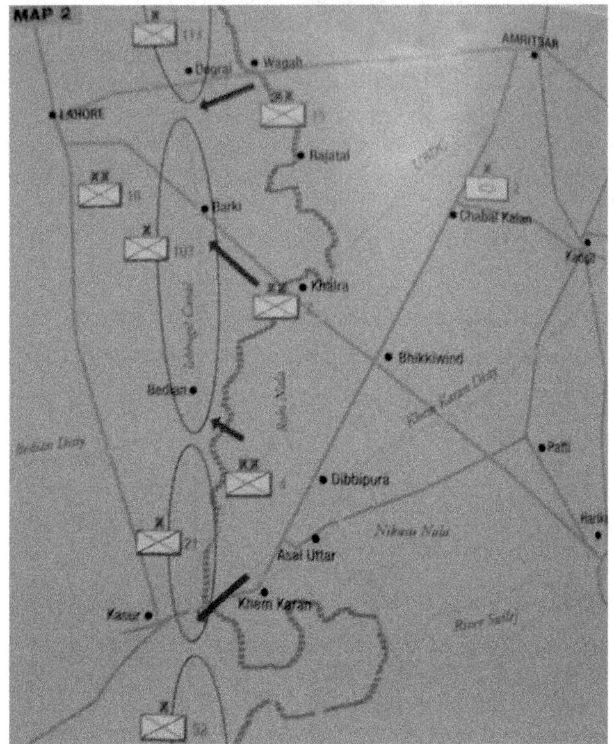

Source: http://indiandefence.com/threads/great-battles-14-asal-uttar-1965-turn-of-the-tide.56928/

September of Year 1965
Lahore Sector

TURNING POINT 16

The Hero of Dograi

> Ek bhi aadmi pichhe nahin hatega!" "Zinda ya murda, Dograi mein milna hai!
> (Not a single man will turn back!) (Dead or alive, we have to meet in Dograi!)

So demanded the Commanding Officer, Lt. Col. Desmond Hayde of his troops after a soul-stirring address on the night of September 21, 1965. The odds were heavily against the men of 3 JAT but the ardour and determination of the JATS was unquenchable, and further extrapolated by the CO who always led by example. They were poised to attack *Dograi*—for the second time.

Dograi is a small town in Pakistan across the international border on the *Amritsar-Lahore* road and is the gateway to *Lahore,* just 13 km north-east of it. The town stands on the east bank of the *Ichhogil Canal.* The *Ichhogil Canal* was 112 ft wide and 30 ft deep and was constructed by Pakistan as a formidable defence to forestall any Indian offensive against *Lahore* especially along GT (grand trunk) road. By virtue of its strategic location, it was defended heavily and even had concrete bunkers on the west bank which was designed higher than the east bank (Indian side).

The background of this assembly of stoic soldiers goes back to the beginning of the month. In order to release pressure and stall the Pakistan offensive in *Chhamb-Jourian-Akhnoor* sector, India had launched an offensive in *Sialkot* and *Lahore* sectors across the international border.

In the *Lahore* Front, it was considered vital to capture identified towns and bridges for the Indian Army to reach *Lahore. Dograi* was one such identified town.

XI corps was tasked to take the offensive in *Lahore* sector. XI Corps launched its operation in the first week of September 5/6, 1965 as under:

(a) *Khem Karan*—By 4 Mtn Div and 2 Independent Armoured Brigade
(b) *Barki*—by 7 Inf Div supported by CIH (Central INDIA Horse)
(c) *Dograi*—by 15 INF DIV along Axis *Amritsar-Lahore* by the Scinde Horse (14 HORSE).

15 Infantry Division at the outset was commanded by Maj. Gen. Niranjan Prasad who was replaced by Maj. Gen. Mohinder Singh soon after the War started. 15 Infantry Division had 54 Infantry Brigade comprised of 3 JAT and 13 PUNJAB supported by the SCINDE HORSE.

On night of September 5/6, 1965, 3 JAT crossed the International Border north of *Wagah*. They not only approached *Gosal Dial* and cleared all enemy resistance (despite suffering casualties due to enemy air action) but also continued the advance till *Ichhogil Canal* and astonishingly captured the east bank by 1130 hrs! Thereafter the gallant unit turned south and captured *Dograi* as well! Two companies of 3 JAT crossed the canal and secured areas of *Batapore* and *Attokewan*. It was primarily due to the leadership of their CO that the battalion did not fall back from the positions which it had occupied. Rather, it moved forward despite continuous and violent shelling. They moved on laboriously under frequent air attacks too. When the Company neared the objective of the canal, it came under sudden heavy machine-gun fire from a grove which prevented any further movement and came to a standstill.

Sub. Khazan Singh was in command of 'B' Company of 3 JAT on that intervening night of September 5/6, 1965. During the intense fire, Sub. Khazan Singh received a direct bullet hit on his head, which though fortunately was deflected by his helmet, but unluckily dug a deep wound rendering him unconscious for a while. On recovering, Sub. Khazan Singh was badly shaken and spotted an enemy machine gun still engaging his Company. Rising in alarm, his boots crunching the Earth and with total disregard to his personal safety, he rushed forward with his gun and silenced the obstruction. In the encounter, he came face-to-face with the enemy company commander and shot him dead without batting an eyelid.

While the ardent fighting was in progress, the JATS came under intense fire from the area of the Canal Bridge, further to the south. Undeterred by his failing condition, Sub. Khazan Singh personally led a second assault. During the head-on confrontation that ensued, Sub. Khazan Singh was again injured badly and much more seriously than before but he did not think of attending to his wounds and fell upon the enemy in direct assault. His men, seeing this astonishing feat, swelled together forward and proceeded to not only nab the escaping enemy but went about dragging them out from the trenches too! 'B' company thus successfully achieved its mission.

Having scored this sensational success, 3 JAT could not hold on to their objectives for long, due to lack of logistics and failure of radio communication with artillery support. No further supporting units of the Indian Army were forthcoming and the JATS were in a vulnerable position being fully exposed to approaching enemy contingent and with no heavy weapons on them. Under these circumstances 3 JAT was ordered to pull back. They still managed to destroy 5 enemy tanks before pulling out when Pakistani troops reached and launched an attack on them with their Sherman tanks.

3 JAT pulled back to *Gosal Dial* by 1715 hrs on September 6, 1965. An unusually brilliant feat which could have culminated in the ultimate success was allowed to slip away! This early victory could have been easily exploited to pose a threat to *Lahore* and would have been a crucial turning point in preventing further ado.

Lt. Col. Hayde and his men had to wait for two weeks in *Santpura* village—deep inside Pakistani territory, before receiving orders to launch another offensive on *Dograi*. Unfortunately, in these intervening two weeks, Pakistani Forces had substantially strengthened their presence in *Dograi*, and brought an additional battalion to support the one already there. They had also enlisted a tank squadron for reinforcements—quite a menacing and intimidating force was up now.

Once the anticipated command came for the waiting JATS, the CO decided to brief his men and inspire them for action with the inspirational address on the eve of the second attack on *Dograi*. If the troops were perplexed about going for the same objective despite having it in their hands earlier, they did not show it—they would have followed their CO to the ends of the Earth if he asked them. Such was the charisma and leadership of Lt. Col. Hayde.

Dograi and approaches were now strongly held by the enemy with two Coys at *Mile 13* and two Coys at *Dograi*. 54 INF BDE launched its Operations on night September 21/22, 1965 and planned a two-phased approach:

Phase 1—by 13 PUNJAB to capture *Mile 13*

Phase 2—by 3 JAT to make outflanking detour of 6 km to take *Dograi*.

On the northern side, 13 PUNJAB scored a partial success at *Mile 13*. 3 JAT—invigorated by their CO and full of exuberance—moved stealthily at night and fell upon flank and rear of enemy position at *Dograi*. They were supported by C Sqn SCINDE HORSE. Every step taken by Indian soldiers was under the fire of at least 8 machine guns from the enemy trenches which rattled non-stop!

This battle fought at *Dograi* was the bloodiest battle in Indian Military history—the first with guns, grenades and then bayonets and finally with bare hands. The JATS had taken up the gauntlet seriously and despite being numerically lesser in number unbelievably made mayhem of the enemy—they were undeniably a force to be reckoned with! *Dograi* was captured at 0300 hrs by the JATS after a gory carnage. What was unbelievable was the fact that 3 JAT battalion equipped with just 550 men took on 16 PUNJAB of Pakistan who were with double the number of men and well-equipped with tanks!

This success at *Dograi* made the enemy position at *Mile 13* also unsustainable and the two enemy companies stationed here fled across the Canal. By September 22, 1965, four aggressive counterattacks by the enemy had been subdued by 3 JAT at *Dograi.* The ceasefire came into effect on September 23, 1965.

The battle of *Dograi* is unique in the sense that only 523 determined Indian soldiers fought against a monumental enemy force that was not only superior in strength—being more than double in number—but also superior in planned infrastructure with well-made and deeply entrenched defences, ramped up by tanks and heavy artillery fire. For a battalion to be able to survive two weeks in hostile territory, isolated and cut off, being without adequate food, rations and even medical supplies, saving themselves and their comrades each day and without losing their minds, is to the credit of their Commanding Officer. Till today the Indian Army speaks proudly of Lt. Col. Hayde, and the respect he enjoys in the eyes of his men is unparalleled.

Notes

- For his indomitable courage and courageousness in the line of fire Subedar Khazan Singh was awarded the Vir Chakra.
- 3 JAT was awarded Battle Honour of Dograi and Theatre Honour Punjab for its exemplary display of courage grit and determination.
- Lt. Col. Desmond E. Hayde was awarded the MVC—the second highest bravery award for his gallantry and inspirational leadership.

I am a Soldier, I fight where I am told, and I win where I fight.

—George S. Patton

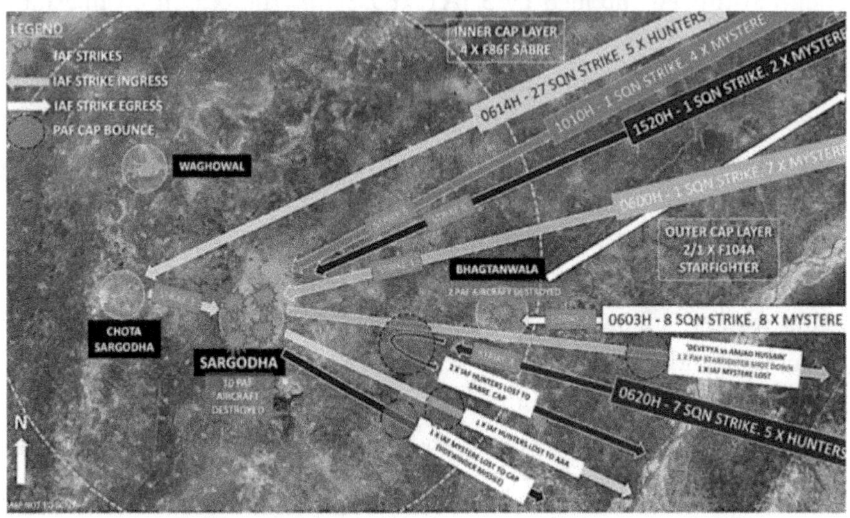

Source: https://theprint.in/defence/1965-sargodha-attack-how-iaf-hit-pakistans-most-protected-base-destroyed-10-aircraft/288878/

September of Year 1965
Lahore Sector

TURNING POINT 17

Good Morning Sargodha!

Sargodha Airbase—the glorious, impenetrable fortress unchallenged from neither the Earth nor the skies—the mere idea of attempting to access this formidable bastion was enough to perish that thought. This airbase rested proud in the *Punjab* province in Pakistan near the *Kirana* Hills and across the Chenab River. It was home to 80 Sabre jets and 5 F-104 Starfighters—prized assets of Pakistan Air Force in 1965.

Once Indian operations started their offensive campaign on September 6, 1965 towards *Lahore* and *Sialkot*, they succeeded in taking away the enemy's focus from the *Chhamb-Jourdian* sector. These bold incursions into Pakistan naturally created panic in the enemy lines. Air Marshal Nur Khan (PAF) was ordered to thwart any Indian Air Force offensive and ensure that the IAF were unable to provide support to the Indian Forces.

Additionally, Pakistan Air Force violated the International Border and carried out targeted strikes ("Warplan No. 6") on the evening of September 6, 1965 at Indian Air Force bases at *Pathankot*, *Halwara*, *Jamnagar*, *Amritsar*, *Ferozepu*r and *Porbandar*. Though they received success for the *Pathankot* raid, they were was unable to inflict any damage on the other bases and those missions were a complete failure due to staunch defence by Indian side.

IAF COS, Air Marshal Arjan Singh sanctioned an all-out strike on September 7, 1965 in retaliation. Preparations began overnight literally—Canberra Bombers from *Agra*, Mystères from *Adampur* and Hunters from

Halwara were hand-picked for the bombing raids towards an identified secret target—*Sargodha Complex*—the one and only well-fortified, hitherto impenetrable stronghold of the Pakistan Air Force.

As exuberant as they were with their self-proclaimed "showmanship" with the raids on Indian bases, Pakistan Air Force was still vigilant as they did expect a retaliation from IAF albeit only in the border areas—never in their wildest imagination did they think that India would have the gall and the audacity, forget the will and grit, for daring to think of even coming anywhere near this Complex. And, rightly so—*Sargodha* during those days, minus the bases inside the Soviet Union, was the best defended target across all of Asia.

Sargodha was unquestionably an inviolable base with blast pens which were considered bomb proof and had an advanced early warning system vide a radar system at *Sakesar* (at a height of 4,992 ft on the outer fringes of Punjab's *Soon* valley). It also had the capability to launch a counterattack of such magnitude so as to blow any enemy machines spotted to smithereens in a few minutes. The satellite airfields around *Sargodha* (main) were *Chhota Sargodha* (towards west), *Bhagtanwala* (towards east) and *Waghowal* (towards north) and these along with the main runway at *Sargodha* were known as the *Sargodha Complex*. It was truly an impossible task to get anywhere near this complex undetected from the skies.

And, of course, neither the Pakistan Air Force nor Air Marshal Nur Khan factored in the will and tenacity of the Indian Air Force.

In India, the command orders sanctioning the strike were out late night of September 6, 1965. And just as dawn was on the verge of breaking out on the morning of September 7, 1965, the Indian Air Force boys of 1 Squadron (TIGERS) were already scrambling for their Mystère aircraft with excitement and trepidation. They flew carefully at low altitude to avoid radar detection. Navigation was by compass and stop-watch only as darkness prevented reading any maps. It was a challenge to fly with navigation lights switched off but the IAF pilots did not want to take any chances. The Mystères team of three zoomed in at *Sargodha* at approximately 0600 hrs. They were striving to fly in abysmally low visibility and were keeping a constant vigil on the fuel tanks as they had fuel just about enough for a single attack. Predictably, and as they were prepared for, they were picked up by the early warning system soon enough.

Wg. Cdr. Taneja was the Commanding Officer and was himself flying in one of the IAF Mystères. He managed to create a bit of a havoc by impudently skimming over the tree tops and unabashedly targeted three of the airplanes he spotted on the tarmac. The second team behind him managed to destroy a Starfighter and some Sabres. Once the siren sounded their presence to the enemy, they made for their exit quickly. As they were withdrawing, they were intercepted by a PAF Starfighter which had taken off fast enough to catch them.

All the Mystères managed to speed away after a hair-raising duel in the skies except for one. One Mystère piloted by Squadron Leader Devayya was intercepted by Flight Lieutenant Amjad Hussain "Amjad" in the sophisticated Starfighter machine of PAF. That machine was on "killer" control once Amjad spotted the IAF Mystère. At approximately 5,000 ft behind the Mystère, the PAF fired a missile and on coming closer at 600 yards opened a 20 mm canon.

The Mystère had no time to plan it's move or turn and was unfortunately manoeuvred rapidly into the Starfighter—which saved it from certain death but destroyed its radio set-up. 'Amjad' (PAF) turned away after the firing and had no idea that the Mystère pilot had survived the attack.

At this juncture, Squadron Leader Devayya could have carried on back to India as his machine was still flying, and he had just about enough fuel to cross the border, but his thoughts were on his comrades on the other Mystères, who had no idea that a Pakistan Air Force Starfighter pilot was hunting them down. The Mystère's fuel was running out rapidly and without radio contact there was no way Squadron Leader Devayya could warn his comrades. Setting his jaw firmly, he pulled in the stick full throttle for maximum engine thrust and went in pursuit of the Starfighter which was now hanging 3,000 ft above him.

He knew fully well that he would not be returning to home base that day.

It was an unimaginable dogfight—a battle-knocked, fuel-deprived Mystère facing a sleek, well-armed Starfighter! Squadron Leader Devayya "Dev" engaged the Starfighter in direct combat to distract him from his mission of pursuing the other Mystères. He deployed manoeuvring tactics knowing that the Starfighter would find it difficult to turn and waited for Amjad to make one mistake. 'Amjad' tried to get behind the Mystère and ended up doing a slow turn and this gave 'Dev' the chance to turn hard and force the Starfighter into a horizontal scissors position. At the same time, "Dev" aimed to get to a firing range position. With his fuel gauge at nearly zero, "Dev" cut through the turn that 'Amjad' was making and got the Starfighter within gun firing range. Coming close at 250 yards 'Dev' pressed the trigger—perhaps for the last time, and the "invincible" Starfighter was terminally hit! The Starfighter machine started plummeting to the ground and 'Amjad' ejected and landed safely—in Pakistan territory.

The battle ravaged Mystère with no fuel crashed into a village near *Kot Nakka* in Pakistan. Squadron Leader Devayya possibly could not eject and crashed with the aircraft. His body was found flung near the wreckage and was buried properly by the villagers with due respect.

The rest of the Mystères team still had no idea of the dogfight and had reached back to their bases—jubiliant with victory—not realising that this return would not have been possible had Squadron Leader Devayya not intercepted the deadly Starfighter. He was declared MIA "Missing in Action" since nobody knew what had befallen him that day and neither had anyone seen the dogfight except 'Amjad'. Thankfully, the other Mystères did not even know the existence of 'Amjad'!

So, *Sargodha* the impregnable "fortress" had been breached and the PAF was forced to recognise the might and calibre of the IAF. The IAF had done considerable damage to the assets of the PAF causing a reduction in the operational effectiveness of the PAF air strikes in the days to come. The significance of this achievement was seen in the Battle of *Khem Karan* where PAF jets were missing and IAF helped the ground forces by pounding the enemy from the skies. This was a significant turning point as it not only tilted the scales in India's favour, it also instantly upped the morale of the entire nation.

Notes

- Flt Lt. Amjad Hussain was again shot down by IAF in the 1971 War and as a POW in Indian custody he recalled his fight with the IAF Mystère giving details of the dogfight and that is how the heroic deed came to light. Sq. Ldr. Devayya was listed MIA until then.
- And, further, in 1980 Pakistan Air Force in an interview to an English journalist had admitted that they had lost one F-104 Starfighter in combat with a Mystère during the dawn raid by the "Tigers" on September 7, 1965. Both aircraft had engaged in a dogfight at low level and shot each other down. The Starfighter pilot had ejected and survived but the Mystère pilot had gone down with his aircraft. As no one else had claimed this "kill" the aircraft could have been shot down only by Flt. Lt. Devayya and was attributed to him.
- Air HQ doggedly pursued this case with the Ministry of Defence and on January 26, 1988 (more than 22 years after the event) Flt. Lt. Devayya was awarded a posthumous Maha Vir Chakra for his act of bravery.

It is the man behind the machine that matters the most.

—Unknown

Indo-Pak War 1965 sketch showing move of
4 SIKH (XXXVI SIKH/SARAGARHI BN) from 06 to 11 September 1965

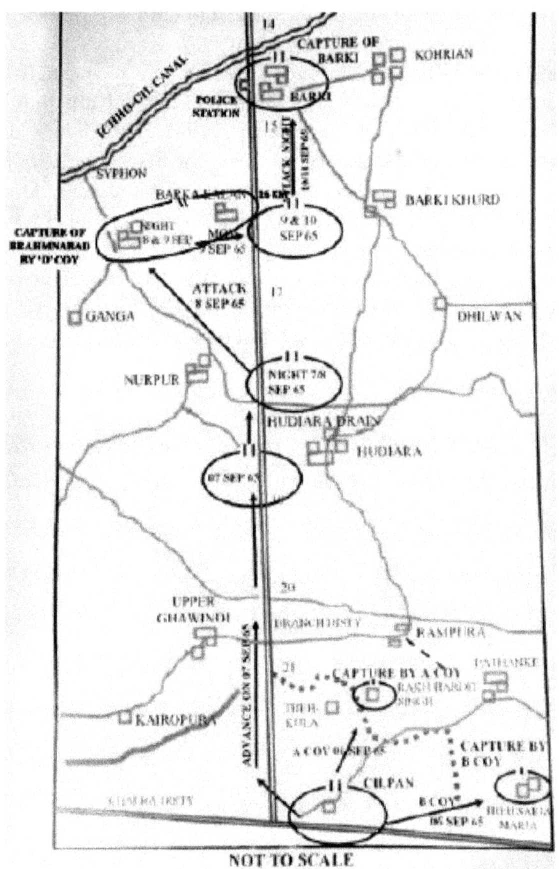

Source: http://www.indiastrategic.in/topstories4042_Capture_of_Barki_by_4_Sikh.htm

September of Year 1965
Lahore Sector

TURNING POINT 18

From Sarahgari to Barki

Visitors to *Ferozepur* Cantonment, which is close by the International Border in Punjab, India make it a point to visit a modest red sandstone structure which has the words "Barki 10 Sep 1965" inscribed on it. Right next to it stands a Pakistani Patton tank and a milestone that reads "Lahore 15." These relics depict the glory of a War won 55 years ago against all odds and unfavourable circumstances and the lessons we may well derive therein.

Barki is a small village located in the Punjab province of Pakistan (close to the international border) and about 11 km from *Lahore*, right on the banks of the *Ichhogil Canal*. The canal was constructed by Pakistan in 1955 to function as a defence system linking Rivers Ravi and Sutlej. The topography was such that its rear banks were higher (on Pakistan side) than the front (Indian side) and was conducive to directing fire on any attack from India. Unknown at that time in 1965 to Indian troops, it also housed concrete pill-boxes which were strong enough to withstand gunfire and cannons. These pill-boxes were fitted with guns, grenades, and other ammunition. Tanks were sheltered behind the canal in turret down position. The canal was 150 ft wide and 17 ft deep and filled with water, which was controlled through dykes on the canal.

XI Corps were tasked with operations in *Khem Karan-Barki* and *Dograi* leading to *Lahore*. 7 Infantry Division (as part of 1 Corps) under Maj. Gen. HK Sibal was tasked to take offensive along the axis *Khalra-Barki-Lahore*. 48 and 58 Infantry Brigades of 7 INF DIV concentrated close to the border along *Khalra-Barki* axis.

Preliminary operations commenced in the early hours of September 7, 1965 in this area. 4 SIKH and 8 GORKHA RIFLES successfully captured a border outpost (*Jahman*) setting the stage for advance for 48 INF Brigade to *Ichhogil* Canal. Initial progress was rapid as no major opposition was encountered till *Hundura* drain which was secured by 6/8 GORKHA RIFLES with tank support of Central India Horse (CIH) after a short engagement with the enemy. Pakistani troops pulled back towards the next major town, which was *Barki*, deliberately leaving small pockets of resistance at each village to slow down the Indian advance.

Thereafter the Indian Brigade resumed its advance with 9 MADRAS and a squadron of CIH. By evening they had captured *Barki-Khurd* and thereafter it was planned to attack *Barki* in two phases:

Phase I—4 SIKH to capture *Barki* village.

Phase 2—16 PUNJAB to capture east bank of *Ichhogil* Canal with tank support for CIH and destroy bridges over the canal in *Barki.*

Barki was well-defended from all sides and was occupied by troops from 17 PUNJAB and 12 PUNJAB of Pakistan Army. The enemy was well entrenched and supported by tanks and abundant ammunition.

On the night of September 8, 1965 itself, 4 SIKH (under command of Lt. Col. Anant Singh) was moved north of the road to area *Mile 16.* A reprisal was expected from the enemy. It had been a tough march. Meals, at times, were not available due to enemy's shelling and air raids. Water was scarce and troops were forced to consume standstill water from the paddy fields. Information about the enemy positions and lay of land was not forthcoming either. These were extreme circumstances for the 4 SIKH troops to operate in, but they took it in their stride.

That night itself Pakistan Forces began the counter-offensive with their artillery pounding the Indian advance continuously on September 8, 9 and 10. This constant pelting did slow down the Indian advance but was unable to stop it completely.

4 SIKH commenced their assault actions on September 10, 1965 from the east—post a rousing and uplifting brief by their CO. They

were in forming position at *Mile 16* as per plan sharp at 1930 hrs, but the supporting tanks were not there! The tanks did not arrive till 2000 hrs and the 4 SIKH bravehearts were subject to intense enemy shelling. The CO decided to continue with the plan regardless and 4 SIKH carried about the rest of the tasks while continuing to hammer back the enemy.

The Indian Infantry managed to hold off the Pakistani armoured onslaught until Indian tanks arrived. The enemy fire was well augmented through their OP by their taking positions on roof-tops of the village and behind the *Ichhogil Canal.* With grit and determination—the legacy of their regimental fame strong on their shoulders—the fearless men of 4 SIKH inched forward. When they were a mere 100 yards from the pill-boxes, they broke upon the enemy with their famous War cry "Bole So Nihal." Hand grenades were hurled around, there was bare-handed fighting, and such was the ferocity of the charge by the SIKHS that the enemy abandoned their positions and ran to safety behind *Ichhogil Canal.* While retreating the enemy managed to demolish the bridge over the canal and saved themselves. In this battle Lt. Col. SC Joshi, Commanding Officer of CIH, was unfortunately killed while negotiating the enemy minefield.

Exactly 70 minutes after commencing the attack, the success signal was relayed at 2130 hrs on September 10, 1965. There were some casualties after this too as the enemy had laid anti-tank mines hastily around, but Phase 2 of the operations had been conducted in Phase 1 itself by the courageous SIKHS, who could not be backed down.

The high spirits and steadfastness displayed by the tank crew of CIH was exceptional as, in spite of their tanks being crippled in the minefield, they continued firing at the enemy causing considerable damage to the enemy tanks. PAF sent some jets to provide air support but they were unable to do anything.

The SIKH Regiment played a major role in the advance on *Barki*, as they fought hard, inch by inch, overpowering every defence. As a result, after a bitter and agonising confrontation the Indian Infantry captured

Barki on September 11, 1965. They held it through the rest of the War despite the use of defensive structures like trenches and pill-boxes as well as anti-tank weapons by Pakistani defenders.

Capture of *Barki* was hailed as a masterstroke - it was a significant turning point. The battle is famous for the improvisation, ingenuity and unorthodox approach that 4 SIKH applied in the absence of tank support. The exemplary action of the gallant soldiers who dislodged well-armed and much better fortified pill-boxes and trenches (the presence of which they only came to know when they fell upon the enemy) was a rare feat, given the extenuating circumstances.

After the War at *Barki* 4 SIKH flew a Nishan Sahib (the Sikh flag) on an old Gurdwara and set up langar for the old destitute residents of *Barki* who could not escape.

It should be noted here that General Sibal had required volunteers to cut the paddy fields so that the troops could advance. He got an instantaneous response from the Indian farmers of the border villages. They came with their sickles and deftly did the needful. There were bullock carts and women and children carrying food for the soldiers and braving the enemy fire. It was Nation First, too, for these gutsy villagers who sadly remain unmentioned.

16 PUNJAB had gained a foothold across *Ichhogil* Canal and the capture of *Barki* provided a secure firm base for extending the bridgehead and for launching further assault at *Lahore* which unfortunately did not happen (due to renegade units). It will be pertinent to mention that the operation was not pressed forward as COAS Gen JN Chauhari did not give a correct picture of the state of ammunition to the PM—otherwise, perhaps, India may not have needed to accede to pressure for ceasefire.

Notes

- The Indian Army would later go on to capture the town of *Dograi* on September 20, amidst some stiff resistance, and come within striking distance of Lahore.
- Capture of *Barki* was hailed as a masterpiece of battalion attacks.
- Battle Honour "Barki" and Theatre Honour "Punjab" were awarded to 4 SIKH
- CIH and 17 GUARD also received Battle Honour of Barki.

- Dr. S. Radhakrishnan, President of India, visited Barki later, had tea with the troops and highly complimented the battalion for its sacrifices and victory.

This nation will remain the land of the free only so long as it is the home of the brave.

—Elmer Davis

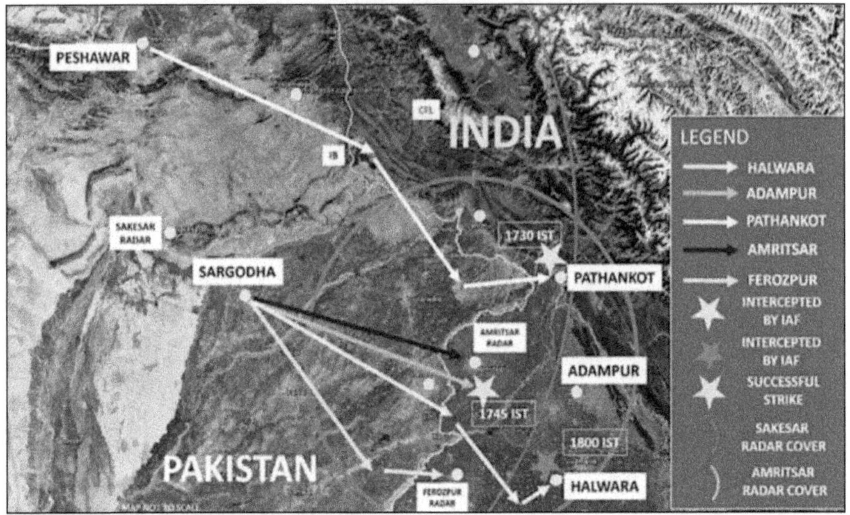

Source: https://theprint.in/defence/1965-sargodha-attack-how-iaf-hit-pakistans-most-protected-base-destroyed-10-aircraft/288878/

September of Year 1965
Peshawar, Pakistan

TURNING POINT 19

The Hero of Peshawar Skies

Circa the fourteenth of September 1965, in the stealth of the night, there was some covert activity at the Indian Air Force base at *Agra*. Four Canberra aircrafts of 5 SQUADRON of IAF led by Group Captain Amrik Singh Ahluwalia were airborne in minutes at sharp 0200 hrs on a top-secret mission. The objective—Peshawar Air Base—deep inside enemy territory. It was a plan devised with pure audaciousness, a dash of extreme daring and raving enthusiasm. In terms of imagination, it was as wild as it could get. The 5 SQUADRON boys were raring to play out the plan.

Just the previous night at 2200 hrs on September 13, 1965, the operation plan had been drawn up in detail and redrawn also when Gp. Capt. Ahluwalia pointed out the flaws in the earlier routing—he had led several covert missions already and was considered an expert on stealth attack missions. But for him, too, it was the Mother of all missions! The crew were briefed about the target only 45 minutes before take-off to ensure complete secrecy. It must be noted that it was considered inconceivable to do this task using a Canberra aircraft, but the Air Force Squadron was confident that it could do the task

Peshawar Airbase was a well-fortified and impermeable airbase in Pakistan. Attacking *Peshawar* was important for India at that time as Pakistan Air Force attacks concentrated on the rear airfields. IAF had carried out successful retaliatory attacks on September 7, 1965 on PAF bases in undercover missions. This led PAF to shift almost the entire B-57 ac bomber force (US-made long-range bombers) to *Peshawar* immediately as PAF considered *Peshawar* to be outside the range of Indian strike aircraft. The B-57 bombers would be lethal when deployed in the War.

Once the IAF time were briefed, each air crew member of the eight Canberra aircraft was aware that at any point of time they could get into combat with the mighty Starfighter (the pride of PAF) —the modernised aircraft with night flying and all-weather flying capability and well-equipped with missiles. In comparison the Canberra seemed to be from a prehistoric era! 5 SQUADRON planned to fly low and avoid radar detection. They had no radar cover and no escort.

Each of the 5 SQN officers also knew that were no ejection seats in the aircraft—pure daring and chutzpah! They were aware of the risk and the enormity of the task.

The 5 SQN IAF team entered enemy territory via *Wazirabad.* With routing and time of action detailed, the crew prepared for action—each aircraft was carrying 8,000 pounds of bombs. The height of 4,000 ft was preset for the bombing—as per intelligence reports it was indicated that anti-aircraft guns cannot hit at that height.

On reaching their target, the aircraft levelled off and opened the bombing doors to drop their load. They missed blowing the B-57s narrowly but managed to set the fuel dumps ablaze and render the runway damaged. This action brought the tracers from the PAF anti-aircraft guns on them and past them (a contradiction to the intelligence reports as the tracers were going well past 4,000 ft). Initially, it took the PAF four minutes to gather their wits and recoil as they were completely astonished and then they scrambled to action. That was the time needed for 5 SQN to turn about and head back quickly (now that they were lighter of their bombs load) to launch base.

Anticipating a retaliatory attack, the 8 aircraft refuelled first on landing back at launch base at 0245 hrs on September 14, 1965. The operation was 2 hours and 25 minutes in total. The aircraft were back at home base at 0430 hrs whilst this part of the world slept on.

This was considered the most audacious bomber attack in military aviation. This attack shook PAF out of its complacency and they were forced to acknowledge the deftness and mastery of Indian Air Force officers. This was a turning point in the War as it succeeded in creating panic in the Pakistan Forces and made the enemy sit up and take notice of the fact that IAF had gained an upper hand in the War. Even the Indian Government realised the capabilities of the IAF and in time to come in the 1971 War, the IAF was a participant right from the onset of operations.

Note

- Gp. Capt. Amrik Singh Ahluwalia has written a book "Airborne to Chairborne."

All men can see these tactics whereby I conquer, but what none can see is the strategy out of which victory is evolved.

—Sun Tzu

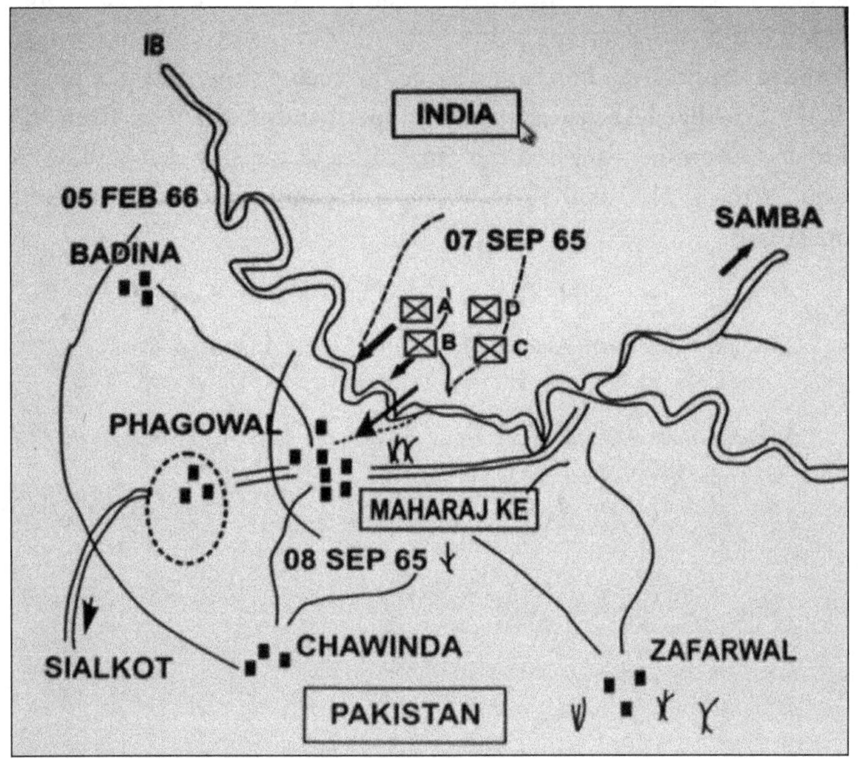

Source: http://www.madrasregiment.org/IndoPak1965.htm

September of Year 1965
Sialkot Sector

TURNING POINT 20

The Triumph of Maharajke

Maharajke is a village 13 miles from *Sialkot* in Pakistan and 2.5 km from the International Border. It lies on the *Sialkot-Zafarwal* road and crosses with *Badiana-Pagowal-Chariana* road and this position gives it a tactical advantage.

As part of India's offensive strategy to take the battle into enemy territory, and to blunt enemy offensive in *Chhamb* sector, India launched the *Lahore* and *Sialkot* fronts. "Operation Nepal" was conceived by 1 Corps for operations in *Sialkot* sector. Its broad aim was to secure positions in *Pagowal*, *Phillora*, *Chawinda*, and the cross-roads so that advance towards the *Marala-Ravi Link Canal* (MRLC), and beyond, in *Sialkot-Shakargarh* sector could be done.

6 Mountain DIV (as part of 1 Corps) was entrusted with the task to establish a bridgehead for 1 Armoured DIV to enable them to launch their attack. 69 Mountain Brigade under 6 MTN DIV was assigned to capture Maharajke by 0430 hrs on September 8, 1965 and attack plan was in two parts. Phase 1 to be done by 9 KUMAON and 3 MADRAS for capture of right half of the objective and block the roads to *Pagowal-Badiana* and *Sialkot* so that enemy could not get reinforcements for the main stand-off later. Phase 2 tasked 4 MADRAS to capture left half of the objective and block the roads to *Charwa* and *Zafarwal.*

[69 Mountain Brigade carried out a night march to *Arnia* (which was near the International Border), the assembling point.]

3 MADRAS reached *Pindorian* at 1700 hrs on September 5, 1965.

Lt. Col. Bhattacharya, CO of 3 MADRAS gave out orders for attack. The Brigade attack commenced at 2300 hrs on September 7, 1965. Troops formed up at FUP by 2250 hrs. Phase 1 troops started advancing with timed artillery fire. The enemy unloaded fire furiously, but the Indian troops kept persevering, dodging the fire and the stream of bullets. There was devastation on both sides, many injured and killed, and soon enough the uninterrupted enemy fire started holding up the advance.

At this point, Naik Samuel Thapan used his initiative and remarkable pluck by crawling stealthily up to the enemy post without drawing any attention, and managed to throw a grenade into the enemy bunker. This threw the enemy into confusion and enabled the MADRAS troops to move across quickly. Though the enemy put up ample resistance, the MADRAS tigers finally had their way. The objective was with them by 0130 hrs on September 8, 1965.

Now, Phase 2 of the attack (for the left of the objective) by 4 MADRAS launched at 0200 hrs on September 8, 1965 under the CO Lt. Col. Mehta. This was a much tougher struggle as the enemy was all guns blazing and were in no hurry to abandon their post. After a prolonged fusillade it became an acrimonious hand and fist confrontation with considerable casualties. At long last 4 MADRAS emerged victors and attained their objective by 0530 hrs—unfortunately, in the scuffle Lt. Col. Mehta, whilst courageously leading an outflanking position was martyred.

This capture opened up the route for the Indian troops to advance further inland to achieve the other objectives of the War. It was a big turning point being the first frontier offensive attack in this sector. More importantly, it signified that India had shed her inhibitions about taking the initiative to attack and was soon knocking on the enemy's doorstep, unfazed by world opinion. It was checkmate—loud and clear!

Notes

- The other phases were completed as planned and this provided the win India needed.
- The regiment was awarded "Theatre Honour Punjab" and "Theatre Honour Maharajke" for their gallant action.

The battle, sir, is not to the strong alone; it is to the vigilant, the active, the brave.

—Patrick Henry

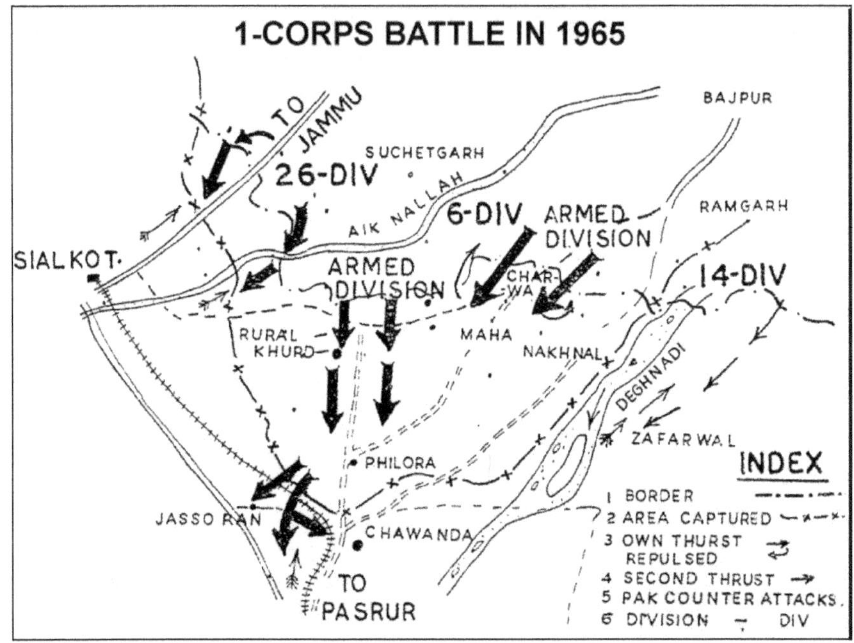

Source: http://www.indiandefencereview.com/wp-content/uploads/2015/09/1-corps-battle-in-1965.jpg

September of Year 1965
Sialkot, Pakistan

TURNING POINT 21

Tour de Force at Phillora

Once the Indian Army decided to take the War across the International Border, headlong into enemy territory, the scale and momentum increased in fervency, and the rapid turn of events only served to egg the Indian soldiers on and that too with a dash of recklessness. September 1965 saw a new military side of India—aggressive, intolerant of the intruders into Her terrain and hell-bent on ensuring that the enemy hears this tigress's roar! Not only Pakistan, but the world too was surprised!

While XI Corps of the Indian Army launched offensive action in *Lahore* sector, the newly raised 1 Corps (India's first strike force) under Lt Gen Dunn was tasked with offensive action in *Sialkot* sector. It must be noted here that 1 Corps was raised only in May 1965. 6 MTN DIV which was part of its formation had never participated nor was trained to operate in warfare in the plains. Its other divisions too were in nascent and incomplete formations. The units that comprised the formation of 1 Corps had never trained as a cohesive force, and met each other for the first time on the battleground!

Sialkot is a city in Punjab province of Pakistan. It was targeted by the Indian Army to be used as a base for further operations into Pakistan. To get there, they had to clear the strongholds of *Phillora* and *Chawinda* after gaining victory at *Maharajke.*

1 Corps crossed the International Border between the Road *Jammu-Sialkot* and Basantar River and began its advance into the Rachna Doab (area between River Ravi and River Chenab) on September 8, 1965. It

had no way of knowing that Pakistan's 6 Armoured DIV had moved under cover to the sector and was ready with a fully equipped strong armour a few minutes from *Phillora!*

26 Infantry Division (as part of 1 Corps) of the Indian Army was tasked with containing enemy forces at *Sialkot*. They launched an attack with two brigades on the night of September 7, 1965 at 2300 hrs for the capture of Areas *Unche Wains/Niwe Wains* and *Bajragarhi*. The operations met with success. And going as per the plans *Maharajke* too was secured on September 8, 1965. By morning of September 8, 1965, 6 Mountain Division had established the launch pad and 26 Infantry Division had established the bridgeheads required. Thus, the stage was set for 1 Armoured Division to strike *Phillora*. Lt. Gen. Rajinder Singh "Sparrow" (of the Zojila pass fame), was commanding 1 Armoured DIV.

On the night of September 8, 1965, 5/9 GORKHA RIFLES (part of 43 Lorried Brigade) had orders to move to *Libbe*, from where they were to hook up with 5 JAT and attack *Phillora* crossroads. Unfortunately, around 8 pm, the rain started pouring. There was ankle-deep water in the fields and slush all around. The tanks got bogged down in the ploughed fields and the plans had to change. The vehicles just could not move, so the GORKHAS in typical Gurkhali spirit grit their teeth, heaved up their ammunition and started walking through the slush. They reached the outskirts of *Libbe* around 3 pm. By then they had been without water for a long time, and had made do with living on sugarcane for 6 days!

The JATS who were to have reached there were not to be seen and neither were the Indian tanks! They had no communication means either as their radio sets were dead due to the rain. Since the plan entailed an attack scheduled for early morning, Lt. Col. Grewal dispatched his adjutant to find out from Brigade HQ the next POA. They were ordered to reach their FUP and await. At 1100 hrs on September 9, 1965, the GORKHAS entered *Libbe* and they could see the enemy tanks lined up on the road. Having great presence of mind, the GORKHAS quietly made a dash for the sugarcane fields, and then stealthily inched ahead to surface behind the enemy tanks. And, then they launched themselves on the enemy with glee!

The Pakistan troops were perplexed and in bewilderment started to shoot haphazardly, but then got wary as they noticed that GORKHAS were slowly building up behind them. They assumed that they were surrounded from the front as well and started pulling out! By 1130 hrs GORKHAS were aware that 5 JAT had got stuck and would not be able to make it but the situation was such that the attack on *Phillora* needed to continue.

Over the next two days there was conspicuous fighting before the outnumbered Pakistani troops made a tactical retreat towards *Chawinda* (south-east of *Sialkot*). At this point India claimed to have destroyed 66 Pakistani tanks! Although 1 Corps had managed to achieve an element of surprise to start with which led to the success, the operations thereafter came to a near standstill. This lull gave the Pakistan's 6 Armoured DIV enough time to organise their defences.

On September 10, 1965 Indian 1st Armoured Division led by Maj. Gen. Rajinder Singh "Sparrow" commenced full operations. It had under its command:

- 1 Armoured Brigade - Poona Horse, Hodson Horse, 16 CAV and 62 CAV
- 43 Lorried Brigade

1 Armoured Brigade launched its Armour thrust through the bridgehead established by the Infantry formations earlier at *Charwa-Maharajke*. Now it moved forth with a two-up formation—HODSON HORSE on the left and POONA HORSE on the right—to outflank *Phillora* with a pincer movement. 16 CAV was tasked to give flank protection from the west.

4 HORSE displayed its belligerent spirit and zeroed in for the kill for *Phillora*. Fleeting forth with abandon and utilising adroit techniques they cleared all intermediate strongholds of the enemy by destroying a number of their tanks and equipment. In fact, the aggressiveness of 4 HORSE troops was so intense that the enemy was on the run till they finally hit the *Phillora* defences. In an encounter, the Commandant's (Lt. Col. Bakshi) tank was hit and he with his IO Ravi Malhotra had to leave the burning tank. They

were stranded in the fields in enemy territory and cut off from the main action. Both had to use their pistols for defending against the enemy fire, and, luckily, got rescued by advancing troops of POONA HORSE.

On September 11, 1965, 17 HORSE of the Indian Army under the command of Lt. Col. Tarapore planned a surprise attack on *Phillora* from the rear. As the regiment was moving forward between *Phillora* and *Chawinda*, it was counterattacked viciously by enemy armour from *Wazirali*. Lt. Col. Tarapore nevertheless held his ground and undaunted, attacked *Phillora* with one Squadron and support from an Infantry battalion. It was a fervent battle between the two sides which resulted in the destruction of 13 enemy tanks. Pakistan Army vacated to *Chawinda* and *Phillora* was captured. Lt. Col. Tarapore fought brilliantly but was grievously injured in the battle. Nonchalantly, with a cool head he planned attacks to capture *Wazirali*, *Jasoran* and *Butur Dograndi*.

Lieutenant Colonel Ardeshir Burzorji Tarapore was born in the family of General Ratanjiba, who led the army of Maharaj Shivaji. He got his surname from the name of a village—Tarapore. Tarapore was the main village, out of 100 more, gifted to his ancestors by Chhatrapati Shivaji. Lt. Col. Tarapore was an exemplary military man and had been in active service for World War II missions and was attuned to warfare.

At first light on September 11, 1965, HODSON HORSE led by Lt. Col. Bakshi commenced its advance. This brought out retaliatory enemy artillery within minutes and very soon the advancing troops were also strafed by PAF. The 'C' Squadron Commander, Maj. Desraj Urs was hit by a shrapnel in the eye, but he refused to be evacuated, and gallantly led his squadron till *Rurki Kalan* was captured. He was evacuated thereafter and the command of 'C' Squadron fell on the young shoulders of 2/Lt. AK Nehra.

Rurki Kalan was a herculean task. It was only days later that Indian troops came into the cognizance of an underground trench system and shelters for the Pakistan Mujahids which was an engineering feat. These shelters and trenches were replete with ammunition and rations for a prolonged stay (somehow the Indian intelligence had not picked this up) and proved to be a big deterrent at night for the movement of vehicles and troops and resulted in slowing the progress of the Indian troops. It took the Indian Forces several days to evict the bellicose enemy fractions (it was a big village of mud huts).

Once 'C' Squadron had garrisoned *Rurki Kalan*, 'A' and 'B' Squadrons made good haste for respective engagements. 'A' Squadron had been assigned the necessitous onus of ensuring that all enemy forces holding *Chobara-Gadgor* were efficaciously curbed. Both Squadrons moved to execute their missions. Now, the enemy realised what was coming and in an abject last-ditch effort reacted harshly with tanks, RCL guns and whatever ammunition they had and sought to retreat to *Phillora*. To their misfortune, they encountered the tanks of 'A' Squadron lying in wait.

During this time, 'B' Squadron under Maj. Bhupinder Singh had gained ground around *Rurki Kalan* and was proceeding for the outlying areas (*Kotli Bagga* and *Dulmanwali*). Though the enemy combatant tanks were causing an impediment to their progress, Maj. Bhupinder with his (two) troops and with brilliant manoeuvres managed to stave off the foes back towards *Kotli Khadam Shah*, wherein tanks clashed directly in a wrathful tussle. 'B' Squadron was now positioned between *Kotli Khadam Shah* and *Wachoke*. 'C' Squadron was to provide support and in the thick of the blitzkrieg they wiped out a few enemy tanks in the area *Kotli Khadam Shah* and *Wachoke*. This sharp and sagacious action broke the enemy's back, but that was not the end. As if on cue, an IAF aircraft came overhead and managed to hit at least six enemy tanks. That was the ultimate for the enemy and they decided to pull back with whatever vestige of valor they had.

By now *Phillora* was being encircled by different Indian contingents—HODSONS HORSE being in the lead. The Indian Forces had speedily eradicated all blocks from the *Gadgor* defences. POONA HORSE (17 Horse) had also reached from *Libbe* and was at *Phillora* from the south/south-west. An uneasy lull fell upon the battlefield. The Squadron Commander of POONA HORSE, Capt. Ajai Singh moved his tank quickly and established total control of the town of *Phillora*. On September 12, 1965, the battle ended in an undeniable victory for the

Indian Army. The Pakistani Forces retreated (and regrouped) to put up a last stand at *Chawinda*. By 1530 hrs *Phillora* was officially taken by POONA HORSE and 43 LORRIED BRIGADE.

The decision to retreat gave Pakistan a strategic edge as they successfully saved their armour from further destruction (this stood them good in the *Chawinda* stand later). The Pakistani retreat worked in their favour at the main Battle of *Chawinda* where they were able to reinforce their strength.

Annexing *Phillora* was a critical turning point for the further advance of the Indian Army, and this success should have been the launch pad for more wins. The continued thrust by the Indian Army into Pakistani territory finally culminated in the *Battle of Chawinda*, where the Indian Army's advance was halted.

Notes

- The battle coincided with the Battle of *Asal Uttar* where the Indians were again successful. It was followed by the Battle of *Chawinda*, where the Indian offensive was halted.
- GORKHAS were given the Battle Honour Phillora.

The quality of decision is like the well-timed swoop of a falcon which enables it to strike and destroy its victim.

—Sun Tzu

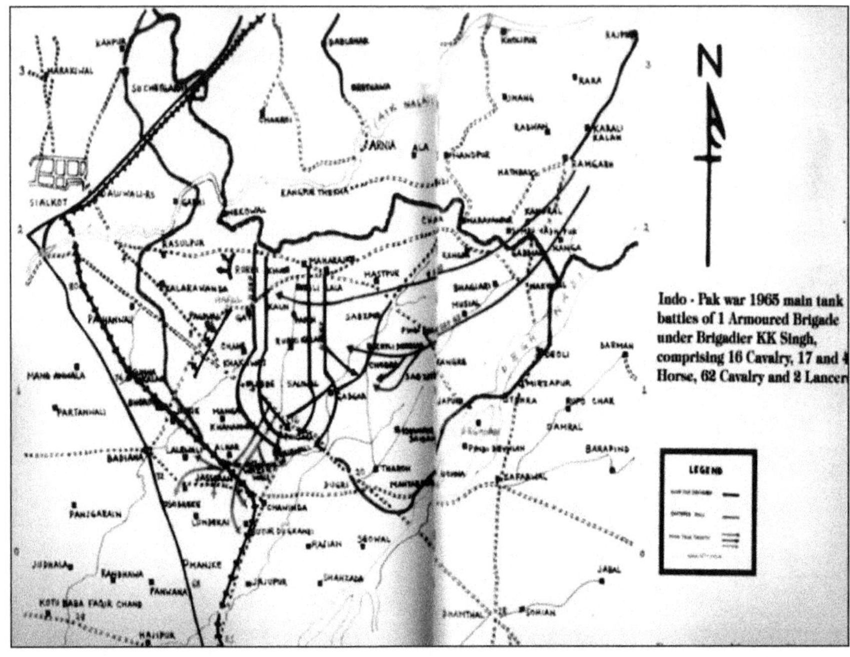

Source: https://www.wikiwand.com/en/62_Cavalry_(India)

September of Year 1965
Sialkot

TURNING POINT 22

The Chivalrous Hero of Sadoke

Columns of dust spiralled onto the rough countryside in the Punjab province of Pakistan, heralding a big movement on September 19, 1965. Thus the might of 'B' Squadron of 4 Horse (HODSONS HORSE) made their entry into *Sadoke*. The Indo-Pakistan War had reached a point wherein it was becoming difficult for Pakistan Forces to contain the oncoming onslaught of the Indian combatants. The battlegrounds were now the terrains in Pakistan as opposed to the terrains of India a month earlier. 1 Corps of the Indian Army had a wonderful start and many side skirmishes were adding up to a successful campaign.

Sadoke lies in Gujranwala district in Punjab. It is located on GT Road mid of *Lahore-Gujranwala* and is on Pakistan's main railway line. Capture of this town was critical for the forward movement of Indian Forces from *Phillora.*

Major Bhupinder Singh was commanding the 'B' Squadron, which was assigned to cut the enemy line road *Gadgor-Phillora* and provide a fire base for attack on *Phillora.* 4 HORSE was part of 1 Armoured Brigade of 1 Corps of the Indian Army. The 'B' squadron unit of 4 HORSE crossed the railway line and inadvertently ran into enemy tanks who were secretly lying in wait and who greeted them with heavy fire. 'B' Squadron quickly reacted, and a scuffle ensued. Maj. Bhupinder's tank was hit on several occasions, but he continued to remain in effective command and by several acts of personal gallantry inspired his men to fight courageously. The enemy was defiant and there were missiles and shells exploding all around. It was a fierce engagement and both sides were equally determined to hold ground.

In one of the attacks, Maj. Bhupinder's tank was damaged and caught fire, but he managed to bail out safely. Despite being burnt and injured, the brave officer went back to the tank to save his comrades. He managed to put the fire under control, and somehow got the tank going again. Very soon he was back in action. He charged further with renewed zest, and urged his men to continue the assault. He succeeded in knocking out 4 enemy tanks. He was a rare officer who displayed courage with the spirit of sacrifice and comradeship.

Ironically, September 19 was also Maj. Bhupinder Singh's birthday. Inspired by this indomitability and sheer grit, the regiment fought valiantly with greater intensity and destroyed several enemy tanks. In spite of having only two functioning tanks, the troops driven by their commander continued the assault. Maj. Bhupinder Singh's tank was again bombed around 5 pm and caught fire. This time it was a deadly fire and Maj. Singh received severe burn injuries. The volatility of the attack had ripped the tank apart and the tank driver was unfortunately burnt alive. The gunner Vir Singh was charred badly and was lamentably rendered sightless. Both Vir Singh and Maj. Bhupinder Singh were evacuated at the first opportunity (which was a long while) to *Pathankot* and then shifted to the military hospital in Delhi. Vir Singh managed to recover, but Maj. Bhupinder later succumbed to his injuries on October 3, 1965.

Maj. Bhupinder Singh displayed great dedication and courage under direct enemy fire by continuing the fight despite having only two tanks after most of his tanks had been disabled by the enemy. He chose not to retreat having the foresight to know that doing so would tilt the situation in the enemy's favour and allow them to regroup—but this was at the cost of sacrificing his own life! He had set an unparalleled example of personal sacrifice and bravery.

Another of his comrades, Lt. Ashok Sodhi, became a victim of Pakistan armour's poor gunnery, when, while he was directing fire with his hatch opened and head out, an armour-piercing round failed to hit the tank but grazed his skull, shattering a 3 inches diameter part of it. He was in coma in Army Hospital, Delhi, for over 30 days, after which he recovered with a new lease of life.

This battle was crucial as it drove the enemy to retreat along *Gadgor-Phillora* road as per planned objective and enabled the Indian advance to continue. Maj. Bhupinder changed the course of the battle in India's favour and this was a huge turning point.

Notes

- While Maj. Bhupinder Singh was admitted to Army Hospital, Delhi, for severe burns, Prime Minister Lal Bahadur Shastri visited the hospital to meet the War-wounded personnel. When the PM approached his bed, Bhupinder expressed regret at not being able to stand and salute him. The Prime Minister never forgot that experience and for the short while that he lived thereafter, he praised Maj. Bhupinder Singh often and widely. Regrettably, the lion-hearted officer succumbed to his injuries a few days later.
- For displaying exemplary gallantry, leadership and devotion to duty, Maj. Bhupinder Singh was awarded the nation's second highest gallantry award "Maha Vir Chakra" posthumously.
- India still retained almost 200 square miles (500 sq km) of Pakistani territory in the Sialkot sector including the villages of Phillora, Pagowal, Maharajke, Gadgor and Bajagrahi. They were returned to Pakistan after the Tashkent Declaration—much to the grief of the Indian soldiers.

Courage is the first of human qualities because it is the quality which guarantees the others.

—Aristotle

September of Year 1965
Sialkot

TURNING POINT 23

The Doyen of Butur Dograndi

On September 16, 1965, the troops of 8 GARHWAL RIFLES were getting ready to commence the march for the attack on *Chawinda.* En route they were told about the modification in the plan (as done by higher authorities at the last minute). As per the change of plan, they were now to capture the village of *Butur Dograndi. Chawinda* being the most vital position of the enemy, was flanked by three important helmets which were *Wazirawali, Jassoran, Butur Dograndi.* The Indian Higher Command realised that the capture of the three significant positions was very important for the ultimate capture of *Chawinda* so that there was a wedge between *Chawinda* and *Pasrur.*

The launch of this attack was kicked off by the GARHWALIS during the day. They encountered harrowing enemy bombardment and unfortunately the CO (Lt. Col. Jhirad) was hit by enemy fire and died a hero's death, fighting till his last breath. This was a shock to the GARHWALIS, and they were extremely shaken.

The task of capture of *Butur Dograndi* was then assigned to Capt. Ajai Singh who was commanding C Squadron of POONA Horse at that time. The Squadron with just seven tanks reached near *Butur Dograndi.* Capt. Ajai Singh found that the soldiers of 8 GARHWAL Regiment were already hiding in the sugarcane fields. They had suffered very heavy causalities and the loss of their CO had led to confusion and lack of control. Then their Second-in-Command, Major Abdul Rafi Khan, took over command of 8 GARHWAL. Since *Butur Dograndi* was held by strong enemy supported by tanks and a larger force, Capt. Ajai asked for reinforcements to renew the attack.

Lt. Col. Tarapore received the message for reinforcements and moved to provide the support with the available tanks of 'A' Squadron. Lt. Col. Tarapore with POONA HORSE troops had been planning a surprise attack from the rear on *Phillora* from *Chawinda* on September 13. The Poona Horse troops had come under formidable artillery and tank fire. Unfazed by enemy fire and ably supported by 17 HORSE and 9 GARHWAL Battalions, Lt. Col. Tarapore carried on and destroyed 9 enemy tanks and captured a few alongside. Despite his own tank being targeted and hit twice and he himself wounded, Lt. Col. Ardeshir Tarapore did not back an inch and continued to invade from the rear.

Wazirali had been captured on September 14 but Lt. Col. Tarapore pressed on with his attack on enemy forces hiding in the area. Once again in a daring attack Lt. Col. Tarapore destroyed six enemy tanks and captured *Jassoran* along with 9 DOGRA battalion and *Butur Dograndi* along with 8 GARHWAL Rifles (after marrying them when reinforcements were requested) respectively by September 16, 1965. Though his own tank was hit several times, he maintained his pivots at both these places, supporting the infantry attacking *Chawinda* from the rear. His exemplary tactics and the grit to carry on was a source of motivation to his troops.

Inspired by his leadership, the regiment stormed the enemy armour and destroyed approximately 60 Pakistani Army tanks, suffering only nine tank casualties. Lt. Col. Tarapore was undeterred by the continual enemy salvo and moved about with his tank cupola open dangerously. One of the enemy's tank shells hit Col. Tarapore's tank "Kooshab" (it was customary for Armoured Corps officers to name their tanks), due to which he and his IO were severely wounded. It was followed soon enough by another targeted missile which set his tank ablaze and he had to bail out. Thereafter the troops then tactfully went to *Jassoran* (well under the command of Indian Forces) to regroup as they realised that with just one infantry platoon, they were no match for the enemy. Lt. Col. A. Tarapore was at *Jessoran* having a cup of tea at around 1730 hrs (beside the Adjutant's tank) when an enemy shell landed right next to that tank killing him instantly! By that time night fall had already taken place and the battle situation was still in a state of flux. *Butur Dograndi* changed hands many times and by last light the village was appropriated by the Indian Forces. However it could not be held for long due to forays and bombings by the enemy. The GARHWALIS had only small arms fire to fight with and it was humanly impossible to continue in the face of volatile mortar fire from the enemy. They wisely took the shelter of the sugarcane fields.

Earlier a message was received from the GARHWALS that they needed food for their men. They had been without food for 3 days and surviving on sugarcane juice only. Capt. Gurdial the 2IC of the 'A' Squadron, took the initiative to immediately react to the request and dismounting from his tank, set about collecting whatever food was available and rushed to deliver to the GARHWALS. He was unaware that the GARHWALIS had forsaken the village and moved to the cane fields (the communications were not functional)! Now on reaching the village with the food he was in for a surprise—the village was occupied by Pakistani troops who had enroached quietly in silence and to his utter shock Capt. Gurdial was warmly welcomed by the Pakistanis and promptly made a prisoner!

On September 17, 1965, the GARHWALIS in the fields were sprayed with sweeping fire from enemy cannons who were unable to locate them properly and therefore had to abandon their plans of an easy massacre of the Indian troops. At around 1400 hrs with a slight pause in the enemy bombing, the battalion made plans to withdraw quietly through *Jassoran*.

There was also the matter of cremating Lt. Col. Tarapore which was his wish (contrary to the established method of performing last rites according to the Parsi religion). Taking the risk of inviting artillery fire from *Chawinda* defences, the Regiment prepared a funeral pyre and cremated their Commandant with a heavy heart. The sudden fire in the midst of the battlefield invited artillery fire from *Chawinda* in which Indian troops suffered a number of casualties including a very outstanding JAT JCO namely Ris Pyare Lal. There was no time to mourn anyone though.

The enemy tanks were part of 25 CAV (Men of Steel) of Pakistan Army. It was commanded by Lt. Col. Nissar Ahmed Khan. He was reputed to be a cool-headed and an outstanding cavalry commander. His genius was apparent in the aftermath of the Battle of *Chawinda*.

Lt. Col. Tarapore's exemplary leadership is the stuff legends are made of. Under difficult circumstances and heavy enemy fire, he encouraged the troops to attack the enemy armour and destroyed close to 60 tanks in the process. This action was a turning point as it considerably reduced the enemy strength which was critical for further victories. Had it not been for Lt. Col. Tarapore and his men, Pakistan would have infiltrated deeper into Indian territory, probably altering the course of the War.

Notes

- Capt. Gurdial once captured had a stroke of luck—amongst his captors was a JCO of 13 Lancers (from the erstwhile Khemkhani Squadron of the POONA HORSE which was transferred to Pakistan during Partition). This JCO displayed unusual Regimental Spirit and immediately took custody of Capt. Gurdial and ensured his safety—thankfully, he was neither harassed nor tortured till he reached the POW camp in their rear. He was finally released and sent back to India after 3 months from their POW camp.
- POONA HORSE was given the suffix "Fakhr-e-Hind" unofficially, which now the regiment proudly adorns.
- Lt. Col. A. B. Tarapore was given the nation's highest gallantry award, "Param Vir Chakra" for his outstanding courage, leadership, indomitable spirit and supreme sacrifice. The eventual test of Leadership of a Commanding officer is his team (unit) performance.
- Lt. Col. Nisar Ahmed did not to know at that time that 17 HORSE was commanded by Lt. Col. Adi Tarapore, his old comrade-at-arms from Aden during World War II; both had been posted at Aden as a part of Indian Imperial Service Brigade, Lt. Col. Tarapore from the Hyderabad Cavalry and Lt. Col. Ahmed from the Patiala Lancers.
- 8 Garhwal Rifles was awarded Battle Honour Butur Dograndi.

Weapons are an important factor in war, but not the decisive one; it is man and not materials that counts.

—Mao Zedong

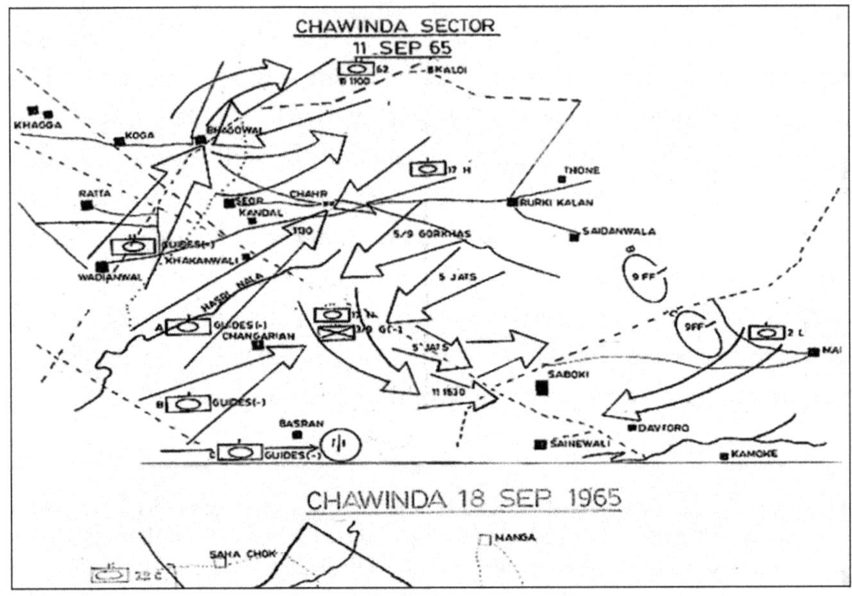

Source: http://www.defencejournal.com/may98/thewayitwas2.htm

September of Year 1965
Sialkot

TURNING POINT 24

India's Waterloo: The Battle of Chawinda

The City of *Sialkot* in Pakistan was one of the cities which the Indian Forces had planned to use as a base for further operations within Pakistan in September 1965, once it was captured. The town of *Chawinda* lies in the tehsil *Pasrur* in Sialkot district in the Punjab province in Pakistan. It is a few miles from the main city and nearing the end of September 1965, the centre of gravity of the War had shifted to *Chawinda*. The area of *Chawinda* was occupied by two regiments of Pakistani armour and Infantry in September 1965 under their prestigious 1 Corps.

Lt. Gen. Dunn was the commander of the newly formed 1 Corps (composition was 1st Armoured DIV, 6 MTN DIV, 14 DIV, 26 DIV) of the Indian Army tasked to take action in the *Sialkot* sector. The aim of the onslaught by Indian Forces was to seize the key Grand Trunk Road around *Wazirabad* and to capture *Jassoran*, which would enable control of the *Sialkot-Pasrur* railway, thus completely cutting off the Pakistani supply line by cutting off *Sialkot* from *Lahore.*

Thwarting the Indian offence with a majority of the Patton tanks was the new 25th CAV of Pakistan Army commanded by Lt. Col. Nisar which had rushed to the *Chawinda* area. The first attack on *Chawinda* was a complete failure due to befuddling of Indian higher command and confusion amongst Indian troops themselves.

The Indian detachments of 1 Corps with trail-blazing captures of *Phillora, Sadoke and Butur Dograndi* now turned towards *Chawinda*. The

Pakistan situation had improved considerably from the time when the ingress was initiated by Indian side, as since then the enemy reinforcement units had arrived from *Chhamb-Jourian* sector. The enemy was easily able to repulse the attacks by the Indian troops as they had managed to acquire additional contingents by then and adopted a defensive position at *Chawinda*. 1 Armoured Brigade, for reasons best known to themselves, had earlier decided to take a halt of 48 hrs instead of using the opportunity to exploit their initial success and advance forward. Unfortunately, by this time the Pakistan contingent gained a numerical edge! The 48 hours halt was the biggest blunder.

"Battles are fought in the minds of the Commanders" Brig. KK Singh who was the commander of 1 Armoured Brigade was already mentally unnerved and psychologically defeated by the enemy's tank raids and in his mind he thought he was being circled by two armoured regiments of the enemy—he was mistaking the firing of Indian 62 CAV tanks coming from *Deghnadi* side (they had gone in the wrong direction and were turning back.)! He irrationally recalled POONA HORSE and HODSON HORSE—both of which had done a spectacular advance without much opposition—and this golden opportunity was forgone in the blink of an eye! Further blundering by the Commander on September 13 again took away foreseeable victory as he made POONA HORSE withdraw from a position (*Tharoah*) instead of assigning it to HODSON HORSE which was the reserve regiment—else Indian troops would have still reached Marala-Ravi Link despite the initial setback.

The plans for the capture of *Chawinda* for the second time entailed isolation by 1 Armoured Brigade from the north, south and west, and providing a firm base for its capture in Phase I. Various units were assigned tasks for the same and proceeded. However, GOC 1 Corps made a few last-minute changes without apprising himself of the ground situation which unfortunately tilted things in the enemy's favour.

Indian 1 Corps had decided D-day for *Chawinda* on night of September 18/19, 1965 (this date was changed from the earlier planned one of September 17/18 due to miscommunication at Higher Command level) and its 6 Mountain Division was assigned the task. However, the approaching cavalcade of Indian troops was easily visible to 25 CAV of Pakistan Army due to the outlying terrain that created distinct dust columns.

It must be noted that the Indian contingent was initially numerically superior to the Pakistan one. A series of inopportune events cascaded. Through a misunderstanding at Brigade level, critical posts which were to be held to propel secure advance for Indian troops were vacated! Commander 1 ARMD BDE failed to comply with the task of recapturing *Jassoran* with some feeble plea and did so 8 hrs after 6 MTN DIV had launched the assault—which was of no use then. 6 MTN DIV wasted precious time securing *Jassoran* on its own to continue further. This set back the entire operations for Indian side and worked in favour of the enemy giving them monumental gains in time and scaling up reinforcements.

6 Mountain Division commenced operations for the attack at 0100 hrs preceded by artillery bombardment provided by 5 Infantry Brigade to the north and 35 Infantry to the south of railway line. 35 Infantry Brigade attacked with two battalions—6 MARATHA and 5 JAK.

The enemy refrained from the attack then but opened up when Indian troops reached the railway station and then surprised them. 6 MARATHA were able to secure their objective by 0400 hrs, whereas 5 JAK Rifle struggled in the face of a tenacious enemy resistance.

By first light, the enemy initiated proceedings from *Chawinda* as they were ready for an offensive now. With mounting casualties, the Indian troops were compelled to fall back to *Jassoran.* 58 Infantry Brigade with 14 RAJPUT and 4 JAK Rifle operating north of railway line while they were en route to their objective, were fired upon mistakenly by other Indian troops—causing them to disperse in confusion! There was chaos and turmoil. At this stage, all control at battalion and Brigade level was lost! The Pakistan artillery had a field day creating more mayhem that scattered and broke up the formations of 35 and 58 Infantry Brigades. 8 GARHWAL and POONA HORSE also came under directed enemy strikes.

It must be appreciated here that Lt. Col. Nissar of Pakistan Army wielded unconventional tactics by deploying an extended line formation in such a way to deliberately confuse the Indian 1 Armoured DIV into thinking that they were facing two regiments and not one! But as they say, "All is fair in love and War."

In all the melee, 1 Armoured Division ceased to be a cohesive force. 500 personnel from JAK RIFLES abandoned their positions. The "acquisition" of *Chawinda* was a foregone conclusion, sadly. The continuous postponements and the sluggish advance had given the enemy the needed breather. Had the Indian troops initiated 72 hrs prior as per plan it would have been a different story.

The only silver lining in the battle was the astonishing feat of the IAF pilot Squadron Leader Denzil Keelor.

On the afternoon of September 19, 1965, Sqn Ldr Denzil Keelor's formation was providing fighter escort to four Mystère aircraft for a strike mission for an offensive sortie in the hostilities against Pakistan in the *Phillora-Chawinda* sector. The Gnats of No. 9 WOLFPACKS SQUADRON were escorting the Mystères should there be air opposition from the enemy. The PAF had been efficient in the battleground—making the lives of the Indian troops miserable by their incessant air raids and aerial bombardments.

The IAF team reached the battle area soon enough and since they were cruising at a mere 2,000 ft, they immediately came under fire from the enemy anti-aircraft guns. One of the Gnats in Sq. Ldr Denzil Keelor's "Keelor" section spotted the approach of four enemy Sabre aircrafts. Keelor immediately guided the formation to take a turn upwards so that the Gnats continue to remain in a favourable position. Then the Gnat led by "Kapila" took a shot at the Sabre nearest to him.

Now the Sabre attempted to dislodge 'Kapila' and took a turn quickly to move away. 'Kapila' under the guidance of 'Keelor' chased the Sabre in hot pursuit. Once he was close at 500 yards, he took aim. The Sabre was hit—it writhed and twisted all the way to the ground where it finally exploded. One Sabre shot at a Gnat and the Gnat pilot "Mayadev" had to parachute out—unluckily he landed in enemy territory and was taken a POW.

"Keelor" decided to pursue the Sabre with pure recklessness. He held on and opened a burst of fire when he saw the Sabre taking a turn. He was joined by 'Kapila' who delightedly delivered another spray of fire and finished the Sabre for good. Throughout the operations, Sqn. Ldr. Keelor inspired and guided his team well. He was a shining example of bravado and courage.

Mystères of No. 3 Squadron carried out attacks in *Pasrur* and managed to engage a convoy of Pakistan Army. Though they managed to knock some tanks they were hit by ground fire.

These sojourns of the IAF on this fateful day did save the Indian troops from a complete disaster. It was thanks to the grit and determination of the IAF that they did not let PAF mess with their comrades on ground and also managed to create quite a mayhem of the enemy forces—by doing so they averted a greater cataclysm—one that was fast spiralling out of control by the Indian ground Forces.

By September 21, 1965 Indian troops withdrew to a defensive position near the original bridgehead. There were no further counterattacks as ceasefire was imminent.

When 1 Armoured DIV had achieved the capture of *Phillora*, it should have sallied forth directly to *Chawinda*—a spectacular opportunity for a sure-fire victory was lost. Neither did 1 Armoured Brigade ask for air support to help as that could have also assisted them on strafing enemy positions as well as providing the needed intelligence on the correct formations. Tensions between divisional commanders too were responsible for the communication flaws.

Ultimately, ceasefire obligations forced both countries to draw a line and end the conflict.

Overall, this battle signified courage and valour at the grassroots—at unit level, but reflected a lack of planning and coordination at Brigade and Division level.

Note

- It has also been said that Indian Forces could have been more successful had they been allowed to continue further to exploit initial successes but were held back due to wrong decisions at command level. *Pasrur* could have fallen earlier and the results could have been different for India. It is also said that the COAS did not keep Lt. Gen. Harbaksh Singh in the loop of communications with 1 Corps Commander which led to poor decisions and lack of strategy—these became more of knee-jerk reactions rather than planned offensive.
- The Pakistan Army around September 8, 1965 had also found the map and plans of the Indian Army in one of the abandoned tanks and had grasped the Indian offence plan easily. Though the element of surprise was lost, the Pakistan Higher Commands also took 2 days to work out a counter-plan by which time Indian Forces had gained an edge. At 2200 hrs on September 8, 1965 Pakistan Forces at *Chhamb* were ordered to move to *Sialkot.*
- It has been described as the largest tank battle since World War II.
- Sq. Ldr. Keelor was awarded the Vir Chakra for his raw courage and devotion to duty in line with the best traditions of the Indian Air Force. He is also the brother of Trevor Keelor who had earlier gained the first Sabre kill on September 3, 1965 over the Battle of *Chhamb.*
- Lt. Col. Nisar Ahmed was awarded the Sitara-e-Jurat for his action on the battlefield by Pakistan Government.

Know thyself, know thy enemy. A thousand battles, a thousand victories.

—Sun Tzu

September of Year 1965
Rajasthan Sector

TURNING POINT 25

The Last Train Station: Munabao

Sand dunes for miles across, sparse vegetation and just silence—the deserts of Rajasthan are so starkly desolate. For years *Munabao* residents went about their lives quietly blending with the stark landscape. *Munabao* is the last Indian village before the border with Pakistan in the state of Rajasthan. *Jodhpur* remains the nearest big city and it takes six hours to reach from there by road. *Padmana* village, which is a kilometre away but in a different country after the Partition, houses many relatives of the residents of *Munabao*.

During the 1965 Indo-Pakistan conflict, Pakistan targeted Rajasthan border as another means of ingress into India. They managed to succeed in capturing *Munabao* railway station on September 8, 1965 and made an incursion up to *Miajlar*. It was relatively easy for the enemy to encroach this territory since lines of communication were relatively nonexistent and there wasn't even enough armour to exploit any gains. It was considered too remote to conduct a battle by both sides though there was a major battle at *Gadra Road*—which is the train station before *Munabao*.

On September 8, 1965, a company of 5 MARATHA LIGHT INFANTRY was sent to reinforce the Rajasthan Armed Constabulary (RAC) post at *Munabao*. But at *Maratha Hill* (in Munabao)—as the post was later named in their honour—they could barely manage to thwart the heightened enemy attack for 24 hrs. Reinforcements also could not reach as the Pakistani Air Force had strafed the entire area and hit the railway train coming from *Barmer* with reinforcements near *Gadra Road* railway station. This had disrupted the railway track.

The Indian Army stationed in *Gadra* was facing shortage of ammunition and logistics due to the supply lines being completely cut off.

Then a saviour in the name of Shri Krishna Sharma surfaced, who was a railway engine driver of *Jodhpur*. He charged up his colleagues and along with other railway staff set about helping the Indian contingent. Regardless of the heavy bombardment of the Pakistan Air Force, the railway staff started repairing the track and restored the supplies. Shri Krishna Sharma, despite the crossfire, made sure that the train full of ammunition and logistics reached *Gadra*. The workers were under the blitz of enemy fire throughout and 17 railway workers were martyred in the merciless bombardment.

This bravery of Shri Krishna Sharma helped the Indian Army reach *Gadra City* and push the Pakistani army back, to reoccupy *Munabao*. It was a spectacular point in time which turned the tide and the enemy could not move forward into India.

However, during his lifetime Sharma was not honoured for this bravery and service to the nation.

Note

- Shri Krishna Sharma was an embodied servant in the Territorial Army of Indian Railways and had an exciting and disciplined Regimental life all along his career with Indian Railways. He served on most critical International Border areas, namely, Munabao-Barmar-Samdhari, Jaisalmer-Pokhran-Phedusar, Lalgarh-Samratgarh sections in Rajasthan as part of various exercises. He had an opportunity to take part in the rarest of the rare jobs, namely, Joint Operation by the Indian Army and Indian Railways deploying Surface-to-Surface Missile "Agni" aboard trains. Exposure to Army through Territorial Army while in Railway service gave him necessary "discipline, courage, focus and foresight to deal with most complex decision making process in various projects," he is said to have quoted before his departure to duty on that day.

The art of war is simple enough. Find out where your enemy is. Get at him as soon as you can. Strike him as hard as you can, and keep moving on.

—Ulysses S. Grant

Post the Cease Fire ...

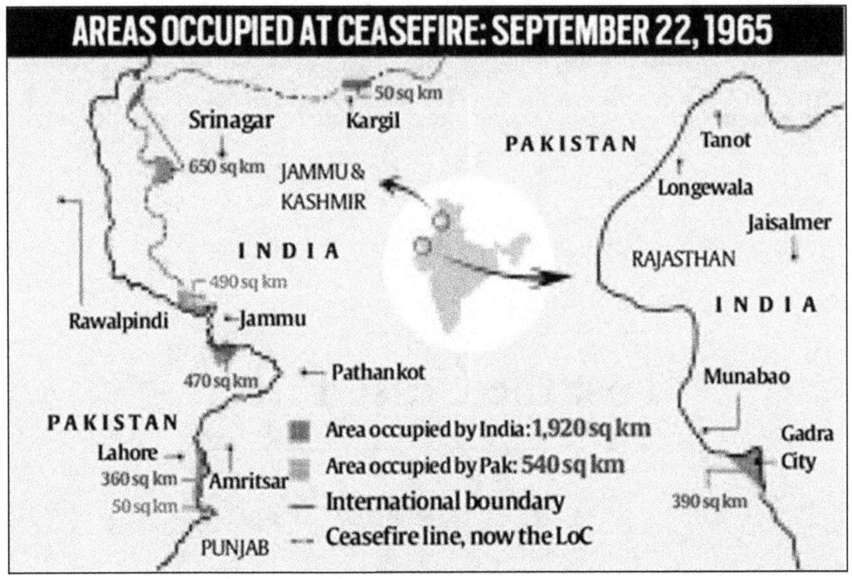

Source: http://olivechats.com/t/bloody-september-the-story-of-the-1965-indo-pak-war/770

September of Year 1965
Akhnoor Area

TURNING POINT 26

The Captors of Kalidhar

Kalidhar Range is a dominating feature connecting *Chhamb* on *Munwar wali tawi* in west towards *Sunderbani* in the east and dominates road *Akhnoor-Rajouri-Poonch* and holds significant importance for the Indian Forces. Post the Battle of *Chhamb*, 191 Infantry Brigade moved to *Sunderbani* area on September 5, 1965 for the defence of *Kalidhar* Bridge to protect the road communications between *Akhnoor* and *Poonch.*

Once ceasefire had been announced on September 23, 1965, Pakistani troops slyly rushed to establish new posts in any area they found unoccupied on the Indian side in the Kalidhar area. *Pt 3776* and *Malla* were two such dominating features located in the *Kalidhar* Ridge in the hilly northern part of the sector. The presence of Pakistani troops on these features posed a colossal threat to *Akhnoor-Naushera-Poonch* road and the *Sunderbani* plains. On September 28, 1965, the battalion concentrated at *Sunderbani* as it was tasked to capture these two hill features to clear *Kalidhar* Ridge. Point 3776 specifically when under enemy occupation gave them a clear view of the Indian Army movements in the *Sunderbani* plains.

The *Kalidhar* ridge has a steep cliff on the north side and since this faced the Indian troops the assault could not have been carried on from there. The Southern side of this Ridge provided a means to launch an attack from the rear, but it was dangerous and risky as the troops could be easily detected by trained eyes. It was also required to capture a feature called "Twin Pimple" in order to get there.

On September 24, 1965, 1 MADRAS was assigned the mammoth task of recapturing *Malla* with Lt. Col. Menon as their CO. On September 30, 1965, once they got the go-ahead for the attack on *Malla,* 1 Madras launched the ambuscade at 0330 hrs.

Marching through inhospitable and well-guarded terrain, the soldiers braved the enemy machine-gun fire through the night. Come morning, they found they had ventured a bit too far and unfortunately landed behind enemy lines! The enemy was equally surprised! And frightened! The Pakistan Army thought they were surrounded by Indian Forces from the front as well as the back, so they quickly fled after putting up a gruelling fight. *Malla* was thus captured successfully without even a whimper. Once in custody of Indian Forces the situation was quickly turned around to ensure no further breaches by the enemy.

Meanwhile, 6 SIKH LI under Lt. Col. Nandagopal had been directed to recapture *Pt 3776. Point 3776* (Point 3774 in Pakistan maps) is the highest point in the *Kalidhar* ridge in *Sunderbani* area (north of Akhnoor).

The modus operandi was that 6 SIKH LI would be joined by 11 MAHAR, and while 6 SIKH LI would focus on *Twin Pimple*, 11 MAHAR would be passing through to capture *Point 3776.*

The battalion of 6 SIKH LI moved along the treacherous terrain that night with extreme dexterity—made possible through the regimen of hours of their training. They encountered volatile enemy discharge from the enemy's artillery but pressed on regardless. The incline was so steep at a point that they ended up using their turbans to twist as ropes to climb up the steep precipice! Poor visibility and unfriendly weather kept them company throughout the march. Sidestepping many landmines, they finally made it to *Twin Pimple* early by 0615 hrs on October 4, 1965.

As luck would have it, they were abruptly waylaid by infiltrators who were hiding in the bushes. The CO was unexpectedly facing an armed enemy with a gun! There was no time to reach for his weapon, so Lt. Col. Nandagopal simply knocked his walking stick on the enemy soldier close to him. This enraged the one with the gun and he brought it down on Lt.

Col. Nandagopal's head. The CO was saved by Sepoy Budh Singh (their radio operator) who jumped in the air in the nick of time and managed to sever the infiltrator's head with his "Dah" (Burmese knife)—swift and painless. At 0715 hrs the CO radioed to check positions of 11 MAHAR and was informed that 11 MAHAR would not make it and the latter part of the operations too was to be carried out by his troops!

The Battalion had considerable casualties and injured and were exhausted from the taxing climb, but they still reorganized themselves for the next assault—on *Kalidhar Trig Point 3776.* With fervour and high spirits, the lionhearted warriors proceeded onwards, and with tenacity and bravery took possession of the *Point 3776.* The 6 SIKH LI troops had been on the move for more than 2 days but still could not afford to rest as they expected a counter-offensive—and it came strong that night, preceded by customary enemy firing which unfortunately also signaled that the enemy was dangerously close.

Nb. Sub. Sarup Singh realised the exact location of the enemy post. In a daring undertaking he took an LMG and went straight across the line of defence. He squirmed into a flanking position from where he could see the enemy clearly, and then he fired his machine.

This astonishing feat resulted in spilling the entire enemy mass and caused them to fire sporadically and then run helter-skelter. Nb. Sub. Sarup Singh had single-handedly in a bold move taken an enormous toll of the enemy. The Pakistani advance could not progress further. This action lamentably cost Nb. Sub. Sarup Singh his life, but his brave deed prevented the Indian position from falling in enemy hands—especially since the Indian troops were vastly outnumbered.

The feature was finally cleared of the Pakistani intruders by mid-day on October 5, 1965. This was a huge turning point since India was able to fortify her territories.

Notes

- In this action the Battalion displayed remarkable courage, determination and self-sacrifice. The Battalion was also awarded the Battle Honour "Kalidhar 1965"
- Lt. Col. P. K. Nandagopal was awarded the Maha Vir Chakra.
- Nb. Sub. Sarup Singh was awarded the Sena Medal posthumously.

- A memorial to commemorate the Kalidhar Battle has been erected at Sunderbani in Rajouri district of J&K.
- Lt. Col. Menon was awarded MVC.
- 1Madras was raised in 1758 by Robert Clive.

The bravest are surely those who have the clearest vision of what is before them, glory and danger alike and yet notwithstanding go out to meet it.

—Thucydides

October of Year 1965
Tithwal Area

TURNING POINT 27

The Kumaon Sally

The Indo-Pak War of 1965 officially concluded in a stalemate with a ceasefire announced on September 23, 1965. But, in the high-ranging mountains, with the many labyrinthine trails and dense foliage, the border skirmishes continued sporadically with the enemy. They aimed to occupy positions of advantage on Indian soil to be used for negotiations later. Pakistan was still pushing regular Army troops in the guise of "Razakars" and "Mujahideen" into India over *Kishanganga* River through *Jura Bridge*, near *Tithwal.*

The Indian Army decided to flatten the bridge to check the infiltration and do away with the route used by the enemy to trespass. 4 KUMAON battalion was given the privileged task. Lt. Dilip Gupte with his platoon was attached to 4 KUMAON to give engineering support. Once the orders for the operations on *Jura* bridge were issued, the KUMAON troops started their legwork with secrecy whilst exercising extreme caution. The commanding officer of 4 KUMAON, Lt. Col. Arthur Salick, planned the mission well and routed the battalion over *Bimla Pass* at a height of 12,000 ft—foraying into enemy territory by marching on foot over 25 km of rocky and steep mountains.

The battalion with support elements marched for almost seven days in cruel glacial blizzards and howling icy winds tearing through them. They were trudging through 40 km of slippery icy terrain and with almost no visibility! Their progress was agonisingly slow as they had to tread each step with caution and ensure they were not spotted by the enemy. They inadvertently came across enemy hideouts at three different places which they were forced to engage with, and they successfully prevailed over them.

The team finally reached the *Jura* border on October 10, 1965 and quickly cleared the area on the side of the bridge by pushing back the surprised enemy when they appeared. However, the bridge could not be approached immediately owing to the very steep and vertical slope so the KUMAON battalion held fort on the cleared side.

The enemy counterattacked on October 11, 1965 and a fierce battle ensued thereafter. The 4 KUMAON troops now ran out of ammunition due to the skirmishes on the way where they had spent their fire, but they were determined to repulse the enemy attack. Lt. Gupte and his soldiers resourcefully used bayonets and their rifle butts when nothing was left and unflinchingly charged at the enemy! During this fierce battle Capt. Karunakaran, Maj. Bisht, and 39 other soldiers laid down their lives. Lt. Gupte was seriously injured with bullets in the neck and later succumbed to his injuries.

The troops now realised that a direct attack could not be possible due to two reasons—one being the disadvantageous position the Indian troops were at, and two, that without heavy weapons it was unthinkable and plain suicide. It was then strategised to destroy the bridge itself so that the enemy had no further means to get to their side, and this would also prevent further incursions of the enemy. However, the recoilless guns required for the purpose could only reach by the evening of October 14. The bridge was finally destroyed on October 15, 1965. This operation turned the situation around by sealing off the infiltration route to *Kargil*. The ceasefire line was also aligned to follow the course of the Kishanganga river.

Notes

- Lt. Dilip Gupte was only 23 years old. He had told his fiancée in his last letter that he would not be writing for a long time. He never did.
- A book titled "Operation Jura Bridge" was released on the 50th Anniversary of the operations.
- Lt. Dilip Gupte Marg in Shivaji Park, Mumbai honours the braveheart.

No guts, no glory.

—Maj. Gen. Frederick C. Blesse

November of Year 1965
Mendahar Area

TURNING POINT 28

The Stalwart of Operation Hill

Once the bugle of the ceasefire was blown in September 1965, Indian troops stopped the forays into enemy territory, but Pakistan Forces did not abide by that. Quietly, after the ceasefire, Pakistan had occupied a feature called *Kaldopi* hill, an artillery post in the *Mendhar* sector of J&K's *Poonch* district. They had taken over *Op Hill. Op Hill* was a 5,000 ft high feature on the road from *Mendahar* to *Balnoi.* This was a major hurdle for the Indian Armed Forces as it isolated the Infantry battalion at *Balnoi.* It was also being used for infiltration into *Rajouri* area. It was becoming increasingly difficult to dislodge the enemy from this post as the enemy had secured it well and continuously rebuffed any attempts to evict it.

Lt. Col. Sant Singh, commanding officer of 5 SIKH LI was tasked with the recapture of the strategic *OP Hill* in November 1965. Earlier Infantry attacks to regain it had failed, so the divisional commander Lt. Gen. Amrik Singh selected CO 5 SIKH LI to lead the crucial mission. He ordered a night assault to keep the casualties down and to ensure secrecy. The CO duly set about preparing for the onslaught and hatched his plan. The battalion size was much smaller compared to the enemy, moreover it was a new battalion—many of the men were inexperienced and relatively new. Lt. Col. S. Singh did not let these facts hamper his plans and maintained nerves of steel to prepare his men adequately for the assault. He led them with aplomb and with a personal example of courage and determination. The men were inspired for action—despite operating in an inhospitable icy terrain, searing cutting winds and freezing temperatures.

Pakistan Army had entrenched itself well and comfortably at the post. They had mined all approachable routes, installed barbed wire meshes all around and were conveniently hiding themselves in the trenches. The 5 SIKH LI planned their operations for the night of November 2, 1965 with H-hour of 2230 hrs. It is to the credit of the CO that he was neither unfazed by the direct gunfire on approach nor with the presence of mines. He encouraged his troops and gallantly led his men in an out-of-the-box but dangerous manoeuvre of climbing the vertical cliff face to access the target.

Climbing a difficult, strongly garrisoned feature and simultaneously dodging enemy mines and artillery fire, Lt. Col. Sant Singh and his undaunted stalwarts in a daring and audacious move fell upon the well-ensconced enemy once they climbed atop—this took the enemy by complete surprise. The close-quarters combat resulted in a hand-to-fist struggle. After a gruesome, bloody, and brutal encounter the 5 SIKH LI warriors managed to vanquish the enemy and get the objective. They excitedly unfurled the Indian flag in their first mission! This turning point ensured that India's territories remained with her and did not come up for negotiations on the bargaining table later.

Note

- Lt. Col. Sant Singh won his MVC for his audacious bravery and the Army renamed the Mendahar cantonment to Sant Singh Lines after him as an honour.

Who dares, wins. Who sweats, wins. Who plans, wins.

—British Special Air Service (SAS)

September of Year 1965
Everywhere

SPECIAL MENTION

Meghdoot Force

The launch of "Operation Gibraltar" as part of the Pakistani offensive in *Jammu* had initially succeeded due to the surprise element. It led to a precarious situation for the Indian Army as *Poonch* was threatened. The only possible way to recapture territory and save *Poonch* was to go behind the enemy lines and destroy his flanks. India was on the verge of losing *Kashmir* if the old road to valley from *Poonch* was lost to the enemy.

In the midst of this quandary, a messiah appeared—Maj. Megh Singh of the 3rd Battalion Brigade of the Guards, a superseded officer who had been denied promotion, volunteered to the Western Army Commander to carry out commando raids behind the enemy lines. It was an extremely preposterous (though innovative) idea at that time. India had no commando units then and nor were there any plans to raise any. Lt. Gen. Harbaksh Singh however was a visionary and a forward-thinking Commander, and given the situation at hand with no other resources, he gave the go-ahead to raise this force apparently without the government's approval!

It may be noted here that this idea was not a novelty by itself. The pages of history reflect numerous instances when small non-mainstream forces carried out subterfuge and unconventional operations with spectacular results. The exploits of "Lawrence of Arabia" are well known and those of the CHINDITS Forces formed in 1943 led by Maj. Gen. Wingate in Burma too.

Maj. Megh Singh quickly organised a force of volunteer daredevils personally selected by him—"A Few Good Men." This force, known as the "MEGHDOOT FORCE" after him, formed the nucleus of the embryo of a first special force unit raised by the forgotten men. Thus was born the elite 9 PARA COMMANDO or the 9th Battalion, the Parachute Regiment Special Forces.

Maj. Megh Singh lived up to his promise and more—he carried out not one but three of the most outstandingly daring raids ever in the history of warfare. His furtive raids managed to catch the enemy unaware. The Pakistanis in any case did not expect anything as spectacular as these stealth forays from the Indians and they had no inkling of the existence of this force either.

The most notable operation of the Meghdoot force was in *Kalidhar* sector. The MEGHDOOT Force was assigned under 191 INF BDE in this area, and they conducted a number of ambushes into enemy camps by swooping in on them at odd times and created havoc for them. On September 19, 1965, the unit carried out one such strike by quietly slipping through the forward lines of the enemy under the cloak of darkness, and discreetly approaching the enemy post at *Thil* which was 4 km inside enemy territory. They managed to administer a sizeable death toll on the enemy.

Three days later they preyed upon an enemy logistic base at *Nathal.* In the onslaught, the MEGH FORCE destroyed the enemy supply dump—the Pakistani troops were literally woken out of slumber and suffered considerable casualties. Then Maj. Megh Singh's intrepid warriors besieged the enemy post at *Thuggi.* But this time the enemy was alert to their intrusion. They tried nabbing the "Meghdoots" and a savage bare-knuckle fracas ensued in which the enemy troops were severely mauled. Maj. Megh Singh was also gravely wounded in this encounter but the MEGHDOOT troops were invincible and after thrashing the enemy headed back. These strikes flustered the Pakistani troops as they were at their wit's end to figure out what was happening and were left baffled and puzzled. They never envisaged that an Indian unit could conduct an assault that spectacular. Today *Poonch* stands with India courtesy Maj. Megh Singh and his special force.

By the time ceasefire was declared on Sepember 23, 1965, the Indian Army had not only recovered from its initial losses but had also captured large chunks of vital Pakistani territory in north Punjab.

The raids by the MEGHDOOTS and setting up of this Force was a turning point. It exhibited clearly that a small combat force could be an invaluable asset to any commander as its mere existence enabled it to undertake tasks that had the prerequisite of swift lightning like action which the larger combat forces would find impossible to manoeuvre.

It was largely due to the success of MEGHDOOT FORCE that the Indian Army decided to raise a separate special forces battalion. Maj. Megh Singh was undoubtedly the well-deserved chosen man to raise the elite 9 PARA Commando (now 9 PARA SF). The Army Commander personally pinned the star of Lt. Col. on his shoulder on September 16.

Today the Indian Parachute Regiment and Special Forces are considered amongst the best special forces recognised in the world, including the British SAS, US Special Forces, Navy SEALs and Israeli Sayeret Matkal and Flotila 13.

A few good men, with the bravado of an outlaw, a dash of flair and hell-bent on living it up with a tradition of valour and sacrifice—the Maroon Berets are truly a different breed! And it all started with one man who said, "Who dares, Wins."

Notes

- For saving India, Lt. Gen. Harbaksh Singh was awarded the Padma Vibhushan and Padma Bhushan both the second and the third highest honours in the country.
- For inconspicuous bravery in the face of the enemy and outstanding leadership under fire Lt. Col. Megh Singh was awarded with Veer Chakra.

It doesn't take a hero to order men into battle. It takes a hero to be one of those men who goes into battle.

—General H. Norman Schwarzkopf

Epilogue

The War of 1965 between India and Pakistan was a turning point in Indian military thinking and preparedness, as it brought out the need for cohesive strategies and procedures in terms of equipment and resources. The Indian Air Force entered the battle arena for the first time and well imbibed lessons which resulted in electrifying successes in the 1971 India-Pakistan War and 1999 Kargil conflict. The War also proclaimed loud and clear that, ultimately, it is the "man behind the machine" that matters the most. And that "the best laid plans of mice and men often go awry."

There were initial tangos, followed by bitter battles with both sides fighting mercilessly for every inch. Legends were created on the Armageddon with units like 17 POONA HORSE, 4 HORSE, 3 CAVALRY, 3 JAT, 4 SIKH, 6 SIKH LI and 6 GRENADIER rewriting history in blood. The Infantryman rose beyond the call of duty and beyond anyone's imagination to fight with tanks! Indians were on the brink of capturing Lahore. There were many feats of ultimate sacrifices, and then some news of abandoned positions too. The unnamed NCC Cadets, farmers, policemen, mule drivers, ordinary villagers, goat-herds, cattle-grazers too earned honours in the battle, but remain unknown and unextolled. The engineers who serviced the IAF planes, the men on the observation posts, the medical forces, the servicemen who kept the supplies going—all these heroes remain unsung. They are an integral support Force in War and these situations were prevalent on both sides.

In the eyes of the world, the Indo-Pakistan 1965 War ended in a stalemate but could well have been India's victory. It was gruesome, ghastly and terrifying—fought in different theatres across varying terrains with innumerable casualties on both sides. Truly, it has been correctly called the "Last Gentleman's War."

And it **IS** most certainly India's victory as She initially defended Her lands and ensured that the enemy's objective was not met, i.e., capture of Kashmir. India's objectives of shielding Herself and then giving a resounding reply to the enemy by taking the battleground to their soil was achieved and hence without an iota of doubt the 1965 War was Her victory. And, contrary to enemy propagation, capture of *Lahore* was never Her objective.

The odds of winning this War were totally against India. This was because earlier under the premiership of Jawaharlal Nehru—a man who reputedly had no empathy or value for India's Armed Forces—the armour was never upgraded for the Army and the Air Force was housing WWII vintage warplanes. PM Nehru treated the Armed Forces shabbily and never wanted to spend on defence upgradation unlike his neighbours—and this came to haunt him in the 1962 War with China where India was forced to fight China without equipment or supplies. Pakistan had received good fortune in military assistance for joining the US-led pacts—the South East Asian Treaty Organisation and Central Treaty Organisation, which were primarily aimed at containing the might of the Soviet Union. Additionally, Pakistan had been making exorbitant purchases to upgrade all its three Armed Forces—a signal that was ignored by PM Nehru much to the country's peril.

Now with Lal Bahadur Shastri at the helm as the PM, the Indian Forces received good support, albeit a little late. His diminutive stature belied a man with astonishing courage. The War was also steered effectively by the Western Army Commander, Lt. Gen. Harbaksh Singh who was a seasoned veteran from the 1947-48 War and knew the terrain like the back of his hand. He was known for keeping a cool head and was level-headed in addition to being an outstanding leader who had the courage and the gall to take tough stands.

In contrast the COAS Gen. Chaudhari was reputed to be a hands-off officer. It was reportedly his wrong assessment of supplies that halted the sure-fire win of India's victory. On September 20, 1965, as pressure for accepting a ceasefire mounted and COAS Chaudhuri's assessment was asked, he purportedly asserted that the objectives of the War were achieved. "We are on top of the situation (and) if we agree to a ceasefire now, the army would support it. The respite we will get will be good to put things right as far as supplies were concerned."

At another meeting that evening, the prime minister enquired whether they could expect significant military advantage if the War continued for a few more days; if so, he would keep the UN Security Council at bay. Gen. Chaudhri counselled for a ceasefire, claiming that most of the army's ammunition had been used and that there had been considerable tank losses. The Indian government accordingly decided to accept the UN proposal for ceasefire. Gen. Chaudhri should have known better. At this point the army had expended only 14 per cent of its frontline ammunition; and it had twice as many tanks as the Pakistanis. If anything, the logistical situation of the Pakistani Forces was parlous. But the earlier reverses had made Chaudhuri rather circumspect, and hence he plumped for a ceasefire. And so the War ended in stalemate. Air Marshal Arjan Singh had advised PM not to accept ceasefire but his advice went unheeded.

This lack of comprehension by a COAS at a time when the odds were in India's favour and his inability to think ahead snatched a decisive victory from India—an unforgivable blunder! Pakistan on the other hand was supposed to have finished 80 per cent of its ammunition at that time! The COAS was also criticised for being over-cautious to the point of letting opportunities slip away. He had panicked when Pakistan Army attacked Khem Karan and it is rumoured that he asked the then Army Commander Lt. Gen. Harbaksh Singh to withdraw the troops. The Army Commander is said to have refused and this resulted in the greatest victory of the War—the battle of Assal Uttar!

There were stories of valour, of men of steel and grit, who had the courage to face the enemy squarely and scoff at death, men who have become legends and then there were those who balked, fled and abandoned posts and caused their comrades to face the fire alone. However, what is noteworthy is the one thing that keeps the soldiers engaged and defying the odds—the trust they place on their Commanders and on each other. That is a given and that bond is unbreakable, it provides the emotional strength and the resilience needed to face uncertain situations. The dynamism of the commanders, their ability to take split-second decisions, the kicking-in of the steady training they have undergone—all these make or break the situation and it is that one man who harnesses his trainings, instinct, sheer will power and grit who turns the situation around—not for himself but for the men he is responsible for. The battle is won in the mind first and then on the battleground, as it is largely a battle of wits where sound strategy is the best armour.

The Indian Forces never leave anyone behind—it is an unwritten rule. The unit is a family that watches out for each other. Death on the battlefield is inevitable many a time. Contrary to belief by "civilians" people do not join the forces to die, but should the ultimate sacrifice become inevitable it is considered a privilege and celebrated.

The battlefield is a strange mix of emotions. It can make a person go insane if he does not have a grip. Many times men did not have time to grieve their comrades who died in front of them as there is always that unfinished business of War to attend to, and no amount of training can prepare one for the aftermath of that shock. It is also this same inner rage that fuels the determination to win to avenge.

Commitment to the military is not for the faint-hearted as they volunteer to serve the country and well know the fragility of life. They quickly adapt to learning to use the resources at hand rather than lament about the ones they don't. Living away from family and friends in uncomfortable environments and without the comfort of homes—under tremendous risk and fear for long stretches of time and with uncertainty requires tough mental resilience and the ability to think smart and act fast.

Despite all the sacrifices, bloodshed, loss, grief and trust in Leaders, the *one* thing that caused an outrage—and has never been forgiven by the Forces till date is that our Leaders returned all the territories that had been won by hard sweat and blood of the soldiers and officers at *Tashkent*. It was tantamount to almost negating the supreme sacrifices that Indian Forces had made to keep the tricolor flying. For many it was a shock and totally ungraspable. The ones who lived through the atrocities and the tribulations of the War, the sacrifices, and specially seeing the remains (sometimes these too were not there) of their comrades, for them it was a major setback and an unjustifiable act which till date is inexpiable—neither by them nor by the families of those fallen in this battle.

The War taught many lessons and these critical lessons were incorporated well six years later when India again went to War with Pakistan in 1971. The eventual measure of success or failure was the politico-military situation in both countries after the War. Pakistan saw Z. A. Bhutto, the real architect of the War, resign after the Tashkent Agreement and the fatal weakening of the Ayub presidency. It also marked a new phase in East Pakistan's demand for autonomy which eventually led to the creation of Bangladesh. In India there was political turmoil after Shastri's death and Indira Gandhi's succession.

Lessons

Despite some of the notable successes in the face of odds, the War highlighted important military realities that remained relevant post the War as well, the primary one's being: Each service had fought its individual battles and there was no synergy in these efforts. The need for joint planning for cohesion to execute strategy in the battleground was felt by both the Army and the Air Force. There has been better coordination since, and the arm of Integrated Services aims to address this coordination.

The War exposed blatantly the limited Intelligence capability of the Armed Forces. It drove home the point to invest more in capacity building of Military Intelligence as well as internal and external national intelligence agencies. (India should have anticipated the Kutch incursion, should have had an inkling of Operation Gibraltar and Operation Grand Slam and should have known the existence of the aqueducts under the Ichhogil Canal and should have definitely known about Pakistan raising a second Armoured Division.)

The War showed the stark reality of inadequate military capability and it was crystal clear to the political leaders that the kind of edge needed to command military superiority to protect against Pakistan and other foreseeable enemies would require massive upgradation of men, supplies and equipment. This is equally relevant in the present context.

The quality of Leadership was the single-most factor that stood out—the right decision at the right time at the right place with the right resources. (In two key battles, Indian Forces captured their objectives—Dograi in Lahore and Phillora in the 1 Corps sector, early in the War, but pusillanimous commanders pulled them back and they had to be recaptured again later, well after the attacks had lost their momentum.) Manoeuvring bodies of men and equipment tactically to overwhelm the adversary is an Art. It requires considerable skill and nerve and, as Napoleon once said, "luck." It underscores the importance of realistic training and exercises during peacetime, as well as the quality of military tactics at all levels.

The War came at an interesting juncture in the global situation. The Sino-Soviet split had just appeared, and the United States was on the verge of initiating its Vietnam commitment. The Chinese conducted their first nuclear test in October 1964, weeks after General Secretary Nikita Khrushchev had been ousted.

Pakistan was a member of CENTO and SEATO, but by now it was quite far gone with its Chinese connection. Indeed, it was also responding to Soviet overtures. Ayub had visited both Moscow and Beijing in the months leading to the War.

"India had learnt a harsh lesson that neither NAM, nor the Afro-Asian group would come to its aid. She was in fact aligned with both the US and the USSR. Given the sinister Chinese moves during the War, it is not clear to what extent Beijing played a role in goading the Pakistanis." The situation remain status quo today, even 5 years in the aftermath.

Structure of the Indian Army

Infantry

Infantry refers to the soldiers on foot. They do their fighting on the ground and engage the enemies directly. They use weapons like assault rifles, submachine guns, pistols, etc. Infantry is an important component of the Indian Army as Infantry units are used over places where the terrain is not suitable for the Cavalry or when the enemies are under cover. Also, they are used for combat in cities and other such locations where it is difficult to use large weapons or mass weaponry. Infantry plays a key role in capturing important targets like bunkers, Command HQ, Ammo Depots of enemies (during conventional/full-scale War). They are also engaged in Counter-Insurgency and Counter-Terror Ops.

Cavalry/Armoured

It generally means mounted soldiers. Earlier this term referred to soldiers who mounted horses. Modern Cavalry consists of armoured transport such as tanks and helicopters. Cavalry uses heavier firepower and causes more damage to the enemy. They have greater protection from the enemies. But they often find their enemies in covers and under protection and so cannot cause much damage. A Cavalry is also more difficult to move and thus it has low range of firing. These troops are used to engage enemy tanks, and also used for Infantry support and sometimes it also acts as a Sapper (Sapper is a Soldier who removes or deploys mines in a battlefield).

Artillery

This unit uses large and long-range weapons. Artillery units are used against high structures like a building or a large area. The weapons include tanks and howitzers. The weapons are towed and positioned at strategic sites. While highly destructive, artillery is often slow to move and imprecise, and used to minimise possible threats before the Cavalry and infantry move in. Artillery is not only a combat unit but also a combat support unit. They provide fire cover to Infantry and Armoured troops by hitting the enemy positions and providing an advantage for the assault party (Infantry) to storm the enemy base. Armoured support is to detonate the Anti-Tank mines based on intelligence or as a part of artillery barrage in order to clear the path for the Armoured troops to move forward without hindrance. Artillery does not go into the battlefield—rather they fight the War outside the arena. They provide cover fire with big guns with ranges up to 50-60 km and high elevation. This can shatter enemy defences and buy our Infantry time to move in. Artillery barrages are used to pin down/neutralise the enemy tanks when there is a group of enemy tanks coming in for the kill.

Mechanised Infantry

It is same as the Infantry but it is provided with Armoured vehicles like Humvee (like US Army), APCs (Armoured Personnel Carriers), ICV (Infantry Combat Vehicle). These vehicles are generally fitted with a 30mm cannon and a Heavy machine gun.

Army Formations

The Indian Army is the second largest Army in the world.

The army is divided into 7 commands presently—6 operational Commands and 1 training Command (located in Shimla and relocated from Mhow). Each Command is headed by a GOC (General Officer in Command) who is the rank of a Lt. General (3-star military rank). Each Command has 3-4 Divisions and each Division is headed by a GOC of the rank of a Maj. General (2-star military rank). At present the Indian Army has 37 Divisions.

Each Brigade has 3 Battalions and support unit and is commanded by a Brigade Commander who is a 1-star Military rank officer. Additionally, there are independent Brigades as well, depending on the need.

Each Battalion or Regiment is commanded by a CO who is the rank of a Colonel in the military. A regiment or Battalion has 3 Platoons. A Rifle Company is commanded by a Company Commander who is the rank of a Major and is comprised of 3 Platoons of approximately 120 personnel.

Each Platoon is commanded by a Platoon Commander who is a JCO. A Platoon has a strength of 32 personnel.

Section

It is the smallest unit of the Indian Army—10 personnel and commanded by a non-commissioned officer of the rank of a Havildar.

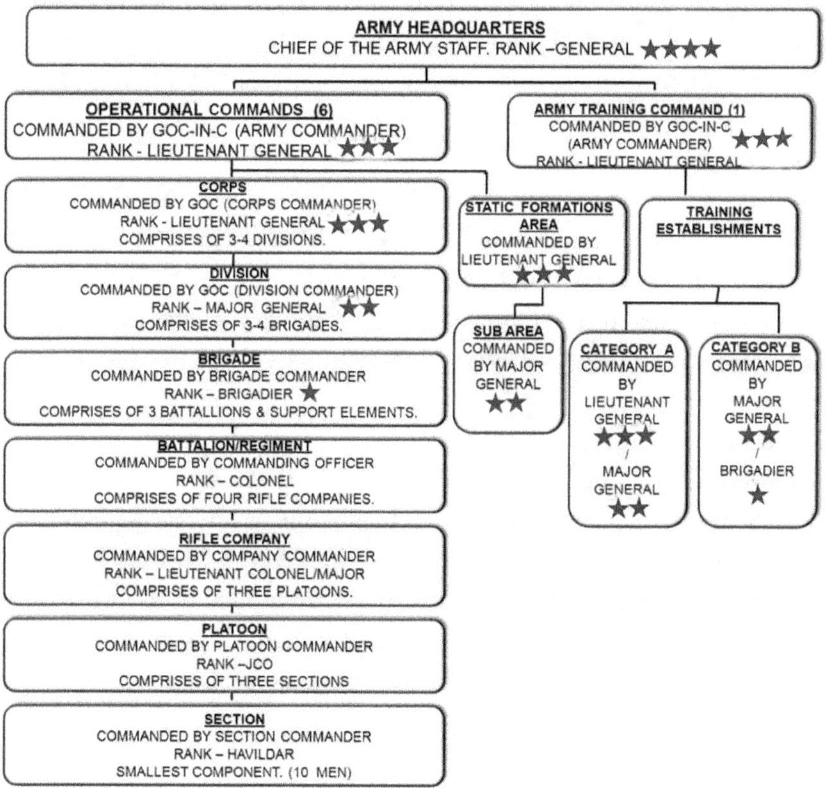

Indian Air Force Sections

Wings

A Wing is a formation intermediate between a command and a squadron. It generally consists of two or three IAF squadrons and helicopter units, along with forward base support units (FBSU). FBSUs do not have or host any squadrons or helicopter units but act as transit airbases for routine operations. In times of War, they can become fully-fledged airbases playing host to various squadrons. Wings are typically commanded by an Air Commodore.

Stations

Within each operational command are anywhere from 9 to 16 bases or Stations. Smaller than Wings, but similarly organised, Stations are static units commanded by a Group Captain. A station typically has one Wing and one or two Squadrons assigned to it.

Squadrons and Units

Squadrons are the field units and formations attached to static locations. Thus, a Flying Squadron or unit is a sub-unit of an Air Force station which carries out the primary task of the IAF. A Fighter Squadron consists of 18 aircraft; all fighter squadrons are headed by a commanding officer with the rank of Wing Commander. Some transport squadrons and helicopter units are headed by a commanding officer with the rank of Group Captain.

Flights

Flights are sub-divisions of Squadrons, commanded by a Squadron Leader. Each flight consists of two sections.

Sections

The smallest unit is the section, led by a Flight Lieutenant. Each section consists of three aircraft.

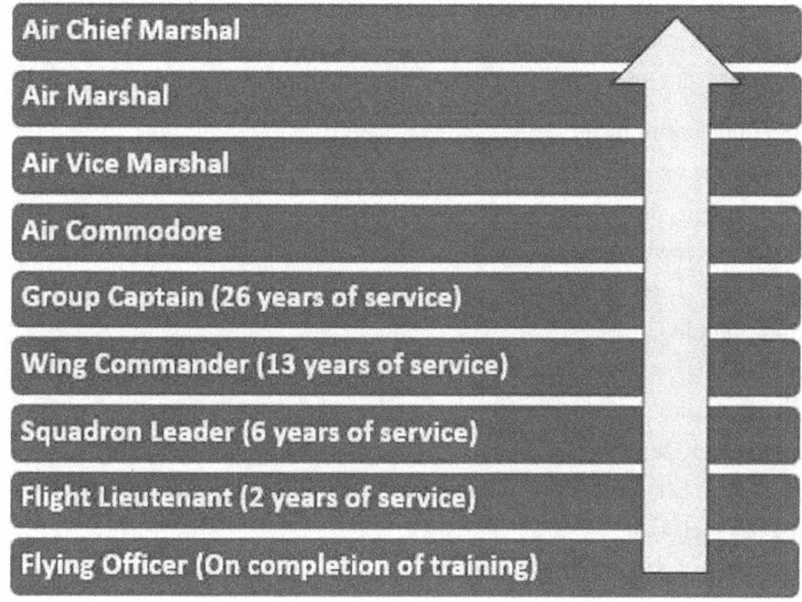

References

https://indianarmy.nic.in
militarywikia.org
usiofindia.org
indiandefencereview.com
defencejournal.com
honourpoint.in
salute.co.in
Indianarmy.nic
Defence Journal—DSA
War Despatches: Indo-Pak conflict, 1965 by Lt. Gen. Harbaksh Singh
http://www.claws.in
Fakhr-e-Hind: Story of the Poona Horse by Lt. Gen. Hanut Singh
Bharatrakshak.com
Indianarmy.nic
Indianairforce.nic

About the Author

Sonnia is a Life Coach with over two decades of professional experience. As a proven sales leader who has worked with well-known hospitality brands like The Oberoi Group, Accor Hotels, etc. Sonnia has built great teams and developed some exceptional managers. She has coached high performers on their achievements and successes and coaches people on personal branding and image makeover.

As a life coach, Sonnia works with people to unlock their true potential and accelerate their growth to achieve success in their lives. She works with organisations to develop their managers to senior roles and improve their performance. She is an avid believer of human potential and is focused on developing people and helping them achieve their goals and dreams.

Sonnia is also a career counselor and is committed to providing guidance for people to plan their careers and build a road map whilst transiting significant career milestones.

Sonnia has been brought up in the disciplined environs of the Indian Army. She is a keen traveller and a food enthusiast and is combining her passions and experience to provide unique immersions for those seeking a different experience off the beaten track.

An Alumni of Lady Sri Ram College in New Delhi as well as of several schools like Daly College, Indore and the Army Public School, New Delhi, Sonnia currently resides in Gurgaon. She does write the occasional blog but what inspired her to write the book was to consolidate the stories she heard time and again at gatherings in her parent's circle. Stories about Wars gone by—the said and the unsaid—stories of valour and stories of great minds—all awe-inspiring, and she wanted to share these with others through her book and pay homage to those who ensure our safety.

Jai Hind!